FROM
THE
OUTSIDE

DEY ST.
An Imprint of WILLIAM MORROW

FROM THE OUTSIDE

MY JOURNEY THROUGH LIFE AND THE GAME I LOVE

RAY ALLEN

WITH MICHAEL ARKUSH

HarperCollins books may be purchased for educational, business, or sales promotional use. For information, please email the Special Markets Department at SPsales@harpercollins.com.

A hardcover edition of this book was published in 2018 by Dey Street, an imprint of William Morrow.

FIRST DEY STREET PAPERBACK EDITION PUBLISHED 2019.

Designed by Paula Russell Szafranski

Library of Congress Cataloging-in-Publication Data has been applied for.

ISBN 978-0-06-267548-4

19 20 21 22 23   LSC   10 9 8 7 6 5 4 3 2 1

For Shannon, Tierra, Rayray, Walker, Wynn, and Wystan. You all kept my eyes on the prize and were my source of inspiration every day.

CONTENTS

A FOREWORD BY SPIKE LEE

Dilemma. I'm directing my original screenplay *He Got Game*, which is about the best basketball player in These United States. The baller is Jesus Shuttlesworth, small forward for the Abraham Lincoln Railsplitters from Coney Island in Da Republic of Brooklyn.

It had been my observation that there was a plethora of basketball movies where their players' skills were too weak to be believable. My numero uno priority with my film was to cast a true baller who looked young enough to be a high school senior. Henceforth and whatnot, I made a list of candidates, college ballers who would be getting drafted into Da League or ballers who were already in Da League.

I auditioned a lot of ballers, but the gem was Ray Allen of the Milwaukee Bucks, my 1st and only choice. As I look back on this joint, at Ray's performance, it still amazes me.

Peep this: not only had Ray never acted before, but he had to go up against Da Majestic, Da Mighty, and Da Magnificent Mr. Denzel Washington. That's like goin' up against Jordan, Magic, and Barkley combined. That is a terrifying task for a 1st-time actor and, as you might have witnessed, Ray Allen was not scared. Ray went in. Ray dove into this strained father-and-son relationship with all the heart and soul that he displayed throughout his entire career. I want to thank Ray for making *He Got Game* look very good and for bringing Jesus Shuttlesworth to life.

Spike Lee
Da Republic of Brooklyn
NYU Grad Film Tenured Film Professor

1

THE SHOT OF A LIFETIME

No one could save us now.

The three-pointer LeBron James missed with 10 seconds to go meant that, barring a miracle, the San Antonio Spurs only had to secure one final rebound to be the champions, while the Miami Heat, the team I was on, with the Big Three of LeBron, Dwyane Wade, and Chris Bosh, would lose in the NBA Finals for the second time in three years.

The writers would soon be swarming all over us like vultures. This is what happens when you say that you will capture one championship after another—"not two, not three, not four . . . ," LeBron said when he joined the Heat in 2010—and then don't.

The fans in South Beach wouldn't be any more forgiving. Many, as a matter of fact, had headed for the exits on that June evening in 2013, which pissed my teammates and me off big-time. We busted our butts, night after night, during the grueling 82-game season, and two months of playoffs, and the team had given the city a title the year before.

Others figured the game was over as well. The yellow rope that would seal an area for Commissioner David Stern to award the Larry O'Brien Championship Trophy had already been placed around the perimeter of the court. Only the identity of the series MVP was yet to come.

The Spurs were having their way with us—that much was obvious—grabbing a five-point lead with 28.2 seconds to go.

We were always nervous facing them; no team in the NBA was more efficient. Every player had the potential to hit the three or break his man off the dribble. The magic word was *trust*. Their coach, Gregg Popovich, trusted his guys. A lot of coaches don't. They leave their players in the same limited roles, from game 1 to game 82. How do you get better if you're not given larger responsibilities? How do you become more valuable to the team?

At the same time, we were making it easier for the Spurs, with turnovers in three straight possessions, two from LeBron! After the third one, and a foul from me that sent Manu Ginobili to the line for two free throws—good thing he made just one—our coach, Erik Spoelstra, called time.

"It's not supposed to go down like this," said Norris Cole, one of our backups. No, Norris, it isn't.

Yet there was no despair in the huddle, and I had been in huddles where players bitched at one another so loudly you could not hear a word the coach was saying. Glancing at the faces, and the body language, I could tell everyone still believed. Without that, you don't stand a chance.

When play resumed, Mike Miller, our veteran guard, inbounded to LeBron, who missed a three from the wing, but Mike secured the loose ball and threw it back to him. LeBron made this one. The lead was cut to two. The Spurs' Kawhi Leonard was then fouled with 19.4 seconds left, but fortunately, he also made only one of his two free throws.

Spurs 95, Heat 92.

Anything could still happen. This is a sport where the ball can take some strange bounces, and I'd seen my share since I joined the league in 1996. Bounces that almost made you believe there were other forces at work.

Besides, we had one clear advantage during those waning seconds. We had Chris Bosh.

At six-foot-eleven, CB, as we called him, was the tallest player on the floor. That's because Tim Duncan, the face of the San Antonio franchise, was on the bench. Popovich had replaced him with another big, Boris Diaw, for quickness to chase us on the perimeter in a pick-and-roll, a smart move by a smart coach.

Lo and behold, when LeBron missed a three, CB grabbed a rebound Duncan might have gotten. Nine seconds to go.

Of course, we still needed the three ball. Desperately. From someone. Anyone.

I wanted that someone to be me. As a kid, I played out these exact types of late-game scenarios over and over in my head when I was on the court, alone with the ball, and in my dreams:

Five seconds to go and the ball goes to Allen, his team down by one. He dribbles to the free-throw line, gets by his man. He takes a jumper. It's good! It's good! The crowd goes wild. Ray Allen is carried off by his teammates as they win the NBA title.

I wasn't different, I suppose, from any kid growing up in the 1980s who loved basketball and wanted to be like Michael Jordan. I knew it when I was 14 and saw him on television for the first time in a game against the New York Knicks. How he ran up and down the floor and soared over everyone in his path. I thought to myself: *I want to float in the air the way he does!*

Only, much to my surprise, first in college, and then in the NBA, I found out that a lot of players, even the best players, don't necessarily relish the opportunity to be like Mike, not when it matters most.

Sure, they are fearless for most of the game—talking trash, making shots from every conceivable angle—but when it comes down to the precious few seconds when legends are made, they are nowhere to be found. They fear they will always be known as the guy who missed the big shot at the end. Get them the ball, and even if they have a good look at the basket, they get rid of it so fast your head will spin.

I approached these situations from the opposite viewpoint: I imagined the rewards that would come if I were to *make* the big shot. And, God forbid, if I were to miss, at least I would have proven I had the courage to take it and put my reputation on the line. That's 50 percent of the battle, if not more.

To be fair, quite a few embrace the chance to be the hero. Except they too often take the wrong shot, the shot the defender wants them to take—maybe a fadeaway or an off-balanced runner—instead of the one they'd want, the one more suited to their particular skills.

And to be ready for the challenge isn't some complicated mystery. It requires what success has always required:

Commitment. Day after day. Year after year.

The second I saw the ball in CB's hands, there was only one place for me to go: behind the three-point line.

Which meant backpedaling three steps, maybe four, toward the right corner of the court. Granted, it wasn't the most ideal way to get in rhythm, but for as long as I could remember, in gyms from one end of the country to the other, I had prepared for this very moment.

During practices in Milwaukee, my first stop in the league, I came up with a drill where I would start on my knees, jump, catch the ball, and fire away. Or I'd start on my back or stomach and go through the same sequence. The point was to develop the muscle memory of getting off a good shot when there's chaos around you.

Few moments in basketball are as chaotic as an elimination game in the NBA Finals, your team trailing by three, the clock the enemy as well as your opponent. You need something stable to fall back on so your body won't go into shock. You have to feel as if you have been there before even if you haven't.

CB saw where I was, thank goodness, and got me the ball. Now it was my turn. First, I needed to avoid stepping on the out-of-bounds line, which sneaks up on you in the corner of the court. No easy feat, let me tell you. I played in

Milwaukee with a guy, Tim Thomas, who could shoot lights out, as long as he stayed in bounds. His first move was to take a step back, which often resulted in a turnover. That drove our coach, George Karl, crazy.

"Timmy, you got to know where you are!" George would yell.

Spacing is everything in basketball. That is why I went toward the lane as soon as I saw LeBron launch the three.

Doesn't make sense, does it? Shouldn't I have stayed where I was, close to the three-point line, so I would be ready to shoot a quick three if CB, or another teammate, pulled down the rebound? Two points, remember, wouldn't do us much good.

Not really. Because I moved in, Danny Green, the man guarding me, went in too, and wasn't in the best defensive position when CB threw the pass. If I had remained on the perimeter, Green would have been right on me. He had probably assumed: *Ray is not going to shoot a three. I don't have to worry about him.*

Of course, there was still the matter of making the shot, and that was going to be tough. I had not been an integral part of the offense the entire night. Spoelstra believed the bigger the game, the more he needed to rely on the Big Three. Of our 92 points, LeBron, CB, and D-Wade had 52. Meanwhile, I had made just one basket, and that didn't come until midway in the fourth quarter, after I missed my first four shots. Let's just say I'd had better nights.

The one thing I did have going for me was that my head was totally in the game. That wasn't always the case very early in my career. There were times, I confess, when sitting on the bench, I felt my mind wander just a bit and I would notice people in the crowd, like my family or friends or a rowdy fan, instead of paying attention to what was taking place on the court. I probably didn't realize it. Chalk it up, I suppose, to youth and inexperience. Fortunately, I learned quickly to tune out those distractions and focus 100 percent on the game.

After all, such a lapse in concentration, even for an instant, can cost you and your team severely. At any moment—an injury, a need to match up against the player the other team put in, a hunch . . . anything—the coach might call your number, and if your head isn't in the game, there's a lot you'll have missed:

Who's hot, and who isn't?

How has your opponent been defending the pick-and-roll?

Are the refs calling a bunch of cheap fouls, or are they allowing the guys to play?

Needless to say, this being Game 6 of the NBA Finals, my mind wouldn't be anywhere else. I had earned just one ring in 16 previous seasons, with the Boston Celtics in 2008, and at the age of 37, there was no telling if this might be the last chance I ever got.

Which brings us back to that final possession, LeBron missing the three, CB grabbing the ball, throwing it to me near the corner, the game, and the season, hanging in the balance. I jumped straight up, as if I were in a phone booth, and let it go.

Whether the ball would find the bottom of the net—and we would find new life—I didn't have a clue. At least I knew I had done everything I could to be prepared. That day alone, I must have taken close to 200 jump shots at practice before the game. From the top of the key, the elbow, the right corner, the left corner. I took shots from everywhere.

I took more shots than usual at the half, too, knowing I would be receiving fewer minutes of playing time to get loose, and always aware the moment might come when there would be one shot I would have to make.

Or else.

Now that the moment was indeed here, the ball—and our fate—out of my hands, I feared the worst.

I didn't jump high enough. I didn't get the ball up enough. This isn't close to going in.

Just then, I saw what everyone else saw: *swish!* The game, suddenly, remarkably, was tied at 95.

Was it for sure? As chaotic as it was in the corner, I had no idea whether my feet were behind the line when I let go of the ball. The officials, looking at a replay on the monitor, would let us know.

When I got to the sidelines, I saw the concerned look on Mike Miller's face.

"Was my foot on the line?" I asked.

"It looked good to me," Mike said.

Except he couldn't be certain. No one could.

Everything depended on a measly few inches. If any part of either foot was on that line, we would still be trailing, 95–94, with the Spurs having the ball and just 5.2 seconds to go. We'd need a steal, or to commit a quick foul, and then pray we'd get off another shot.

There was nothing to fear. I was well behind the line. The fans, those who hadn't given up on us, went nuts. People in the parking lot, I found out later, tried to get back in but couldn't.

From then on, we took advantage, stopping the Spurs on their final possession—Tony Parker missed a fadeaway—and outscoring them 8–5 in overtime to win, 103–100. No one was happier than LeBron.

"Thank you, Jesus," he said. "Thank you, Jesus." He was referring to Jesus Shuttlesworth, the character I played in Spike Lee's film *He Got Game,* back in the late '90s.

"I'm just glad I could play my part," I told him.

Two nights later, in the deciding Game 7, we survived another close one, 95–88, LeBron leading the way with 37 points, including five threes, and 12 rebounds. Shane Battier, our backup forward, also came up big, nailing six of eight threes. I didn't score a single point but couldn't have cared less. I scored the three points we had to have in Game 6, and we were the world champions.

Was I thrilled to win a second ring? Absolutely. Is there any better feeling in sports? Hell no.

Yet, as rewarding as it felt to be in the locker room after Game 7—the champagne and tears flowing, the deep sigh of relief—the real victory didn't come that night. The victory came on other nights, one after another, when there were no fans or cameras.

Just me and the ball.

When I ran into Mark Cuban, the Dallas Mavericks owner, in 2016, he paid me a wonderful compliment.

Mark didn't bring up how many threes I made or how many records I set. He said that when the team I was on came to Dallas, he would walk into the gym a few hours before the game to watch me go through my routine. That, he told me, is what he'll cherish most about my career. That is what I'll cherish most too.

The games are beyond my control, which isn't the case when I'm by myself. In these moments, I'm in control of the shots I'll take, of the moves I'll try, of how much I'll run. I'm never more at peace.

It reminds me of the days I spent a lifetime ago in the small town of Dalzell, South Carolina, when basketball was a sign of light and hope in a dark and confusing world.

2

GO SOUTH, YOUNG MAN

Growing up, I never felt as if I truly belonged.

How could I? My dad, Walter Allen, served as a metal technician in the United States Air Force, which meant we moved a lot—from Northern California, where I was born on July 20, 1975, to Germany to Oklahoma to England to Southern California to, in the fall of 1988, Dalzell, roughly 40 miles from Columbia, the state capital. It was no surprise that, by the time I made it to the NBA in the mid-1990s, I was used to life on the road.

I couldn't be more grateful for that kind of life. I was able to visit places most of us never see, and it helped me understand that, as proud as I am to be an American, we don't have a monopoly on the right way to think and live. The British have their own perspective, as do the Germans, as do dozens of other societies across the globe. This may be difficult for some back home to comprehend, but the world doesn't revolve around the United States of America.

On the other hand, there are serious downsides to such a nomadic existence, even if you end up in the most beautiful locations. For me, the saddest part was feeling as if I was always letting go of something I deeply valued. What would be the point of committing to anything? It would soon be gone anyway.

I tried to get along with the other kids, hoping they would realize I was no different than anybody else, but even when we bonded, the moment would come every two or three years for me, or them, to move on to the next posting. You could say I was traded over and over and over by the same general manager, Uncle Sam, and wherever he ordered us to go, I would have to start from scratch. It hit me hard every time.

Never did I feel as much an outsider as when we set foot for the first time in South Carolina . . . *the South*.

The state was the first to secede from the Union in late 1860, leading to the Civil War—the war that some, more than 120 years after Lee surrendered to Grant, were still fighting, with words if not weapons.

It was difficult enough to be plopped down in a part of the nation I knew little about, but it was also a couple of months after the school year had gotten under way. Those months made a huge difference. The cliques had been formed, the judgments, even if rash, made. Now here comes this new kid from somewhere out west. Seriously, what chance did I have to fit in?

I wasn't the only one in the Allen household who had trouble making the adjustment this time.

When my mother dropped me off on my first day of eighth grade at Ebenezer Junior High, she burst into tears as she noticed how run-down and dirty the school was and that it was across the street from a cemetery.

Driving a little farther down the block, you ran into farms, one after another, and woods. We were living in the country, no getting around it, and in some ways, it felt like living in the past. Nothing against the country—there were a lot of wonderful people in those parts—but it was a very tough transition for us, and while we were there to serve, my mom felt guilty, as any parent would.

To give you a sense of what we had to deal with, the drinking water in the fountains at Ebenezer came out orange at first because of the rusty pipes. You drank it anyway. Unless you wanted to go thirsty for the rest of the day.

Even so, my siblings and I didn't complain. That's probably because, from the time I could first remember, we didn't have very much. The government paid for our housing, but every other expense was left to us.

Other families in Dalzell, to be fair, had it just as bad, but because there were five kids in our family —I was the middle child—there was less of everything to go around. I walked with holes in my shoes and put clothes on layaway. On occasion, I wore stuff handed down from my brother, John, who was three years older, but I grew so fast, nothing fit for long. All of us knew every two weeks when it was payday; it meant there would be groceries, which we stretched out for as many days as we could.

You found a way to get by, simple as that, which had

also been the case when we lived in California. Back then, though, there was one time I let our situation get to me and made a terrible mistake. I was 11 or 12 years old when I went into the grocery store on the base and stole a box of licorice. I was hungry and knew better than to ask my mom for money we didn't have. I carefully hid the licorice in the sleeve of my jacket and walked to the door, thinking I was so damn clever.

I was an idiot. The clerk behind the counter was in my face quicker than Gary Payton. The police soon arrived and put me in the back of a cruiser to take me to the station.

Before I knew it, I was sitting on a chair in a small room that didn't have any windows. The minutes felt like hours. I was scared to death. All for a lousy box of licorice.

The crazy thing is, the cops didn't scare me. My parents did. I would rather have been arrested than have to deal with them.

First Mom, who, whenever I'd acted up before, didn't hesitate to use a belt. She didn't have to say much this time. The look of disappointment she gave me was enough.

"I can't believe you did this," she told me. "I can't wait until your dad comes home."

That's where I lucked out. Dad was serving in South Korea on a one-year tour. Come to think of it, that might very well be why I also took the risk in the first place. He couldn't spank me with a belt, his typical form of punishment, from 7,000 miles away.

Yell at me, that he could do, and I couldn't blame him. Because of what I had done, there was a chance he would lose one of his stripes, and stripes meant everything in the armed forces.

Thank God he didn't. I would never have forgiven myself. By the time he came home two months later, all was forgotten. All except the lesson I learned: don't ever take anything that doesn't belong to you.

There were other lessons growing up, some just as painful.

Once in South Carolina a friend told me I could borrow a pair of his shorts, which he would bring over to my house the night before school. I needed them badly. For weeks, I had been going back and forth between the same two pairs of jeans. The other kids noticed and didn't hesitate to let me hear about it. I'd show them. I would walk down the halls of Ebenezer Junior High wearing my new shorts, and no one would be able to make fun of me.

I sat by the window that night and waited for my friend, and waited . . . and waited.

He never showed up. Whatever his excuse was, I don't remember. All I remember is how determined I was that the day would come, sooner rather than later, when I wouldn't have to depend on anyone ever again, for anything. That included my parents, especially my father. As tight as money was in our house, he could have helped out more.

Countless mornings, around five o'clock, I was awoken when he pulled into the driveway after being out with his friends all night. I was constantly amazed how he'd still be ready to go to work a few hours later, as if he'd been asleep the whole time. Even so, the money he spent meant there would be none left for me to buy food in the school cafeteria.

"Why don't you have lunch?" the other kids used to ask.

"I'm not hungry," I said.

I thought it was better to lie—to them and, I suppose,

to myself—than to put up with more humiliation; I was still getting my share from wearing the same two pairs of jeans.

My father, it needs to be pointed out, was respected by everyone at work, and the men he supervised learned a great deal from him. Nonetheless, as smart as he was, he didn't advance in his career as far as he could have. I made a promise to myself right then and there: *whatever job I get when I grow up, I'll work as hard as I can.* No matter how I felt about some of the choices he made, he was my father, and I loved him.

Mom, on the other hand, wasn't always as understanding, and one time she paid for it. She and my father were having an argument when he got a little physical with her. I tried to force my way between them, but he was rough with me as well. I was 13 years old. I didn't stand a chance.

Why did my mother stay with him? Well, they did separate, a couple of times. When my father went off to Korea, on two separate tours, the reason that we didn't go with him, my siblings and I suspected, was because he and Mom wanted to determine if the time away from each other might do the marriage some good. Whether it did or not, I have no clue. I don't recall any changes in how they treated each other when he got back, but I was hardly the best judge.

Our financial situation, I have to believe, played a role in her trying to patch things up. Whatever he did with his evenings, he brought home a paycheck every two weeks, and with so many mouths to feed, that was not to be taken lightly.

Even with her other responsibilities Mom somehow found time to work two jobs: as a cashier at a gas station, and cleaning homes on the base after the residents had moved out. She went through every inch of the place: scrubbing the toilets, walls, and floors, and washing the baseboards, the rest of the family pitching in. The extra cash she brought in made a huge difference.

She was no stranger to hard work, that's for sure. Growing up in rural Arkansas during the late '50s, she used to rush out to the fields to help her parents and siblings pick cotton as soon as she got home from school.

Earlier, in California, I made some money of my own, by mowing lawns.

That was a big deal at Edwards Air Force Base, with the inspections they held every Thursday. You weren't allowed to let the grass grow on the sidewalks, through the cracks, or you'd get written up. From walking around the neighborhood, I kept track of which folks cut their grass and which ones paid someone to do it.

Needless to say, I wasn't the only kid on the base with this brilliant idea, which meant I would have to stand out from everyone else. So each Wednesday afternoon, on my way to knock on people's doors, I rehearsed precisely what I was going to say.

I didn't make a fortune—10 bucks a lawn—but I could usually finish in a half-hour or so and get to five houses before it got dark. That was 50 bucks, an honest day's work, which was enough to buy candy and other goodies at the store.

Prior to South Carolina, in the States or abroad, my siblings and I went to the schools on the base, where there were basketball courts, tennis courts, and plenty of other amenities. You almost felt you were on a college campus. With the Defense Department paying for everything, you would expect nothing less than spotless in the classrooms and hallways. They gave us the best of everything: the best programs, the best textbooks, and, most important, the best teachers. These teachers, well paid and highly respected, cared a lot about their students, doing whatever they could to get them ready for the challenges ahead.

That wasn't the situation at Ebenezer, or at Hillcrest High, a few miles down the road, where I went afterward.

The teachers were not well paid and didn't have anywhere near the same resources. They cared about us, although some would flunk you without giving it a second thought. I often think of what some of those kids might have done with their lives, if only someone had believed in them instead of giving up on them. That goes for a few of the coaches as well.

Take my brother, John. He was one of the state's top running backs his senior year, and this was, remember, the *South,* where football was, and always will be, a religion. His grades weren't the best, but John was a very bright kid. Yet, instead of waiting to see if he could bring those grades up, one of the coaches spread the word that John wouldn't graduate with his class. He had no way of knowing that. The recruiters stopped checking in on him, and my brother never did make it to college, which has changed the course of his life. For the record, he graduated on time.

The teachers at Ebenezer had a lot to deal with, though. To this day, I've never heard as many four-letter words as I did from the kids in junior high, and being around the game of basketball for as long as I was, with the pushing and shoving and constant challenges to one's manhood, I was exposed to plenty of profane language.

Then there was the drinking and the drugs and the

sex—and to think, we weren't in high school yet, when the hormones would kick in even more. One girl in my eighth-grade class was pregnant, and yet no one appeared to think it was out of the ordinary. I suppose that says a lot about the times we were living in.

Despite needing to adjust to a new culture, I did my best to learn as much as I could, even if some of what I learned was quite disturbing.

Exhibit A: American History.

In history classes I took in California, I learned about Abraham Lincoln, Teddy Roosevelt, John Kennedy, and other leaders from our country's past, and I expected more of the same at Ebenezer. Instead, I learned about leaders from South Carolina's past, men who could never be leaders to me, and a lot of black folks.

They included John C. Calhoun, the former senator and vice president from the 1800s . . . and slave owner! No, the teachers did not tell us about *that* John C. Calhoun; I would discover the truth on my own later. Still, I didn't complain to anyone at school or say a word to my parents. They had enough to deal with without me adding to their burdens.

Far from being ashamed of the state's racist past—and present, you could argue—the teachers glorified it, no matter how much agony the institution of slavery caused to so many, for so long. What could you expect, I suppose, from a place that kept electing Senator Strom Thurmond, a fierce opponent of integration, into his nineties? Where the Confederate flag hung from the top of the statehouse?

Just a couple of blocks from our home, as a matter of fact, stood a large housing development known as Oakland Plantation. The actual plantation home was still intact, including the shackles hanging on the walls. It was creepy, but we were too young to fully grasp what it meant. I get chills every time I think about those shackles now. After what took place in Charlottesville in 2017, we've come to see how important it is to take down these symbols of oppression, wherever they might stand. Better late than never.

Back then, for me, it wasn't just black versus white. Some of the black people looked down on me too, and it wasn't merely because I was the new kid. I also made the mistake of speaking the wrong way.

"You talk like a white boy," they kept telling me.

White boy?

That was something I had not heard before, and it made me upset and confused. I was speaking the way I had always spoken. I had no idea what black people were *supposed* to sound like. Wherever we were posted, I never thought of color in how I identified myself or those I hung around with. We served with other Americans. Not white or black Americans.

Naturally, kids being kids, they could be incredibly insensitive at times, and because I didn't know anyone in South Carolina and, as usual, hoped to fit in, I was susceptible to any criticism from peers. For the first time, I began to question my very being: Was there something wrong with me? Should I be like them?

Speaking in a different way wasn't my only crime. So was having the nerve to be friends with white boys and girls, even if they happened to live right next door, which never made sense to me. Just because I played hide-and-seek with a white kid didn't mean I was white.

It wasn't like that in California.

Remember the film *Stand by Me*, starring River Phoenix and Corey Feldman, with the classic Ben E. King song from the early 1960s playing in the background? The boys I knew at Edwards, black and white, were just like those boys in the film.

We camped out in one another's backyards; went fishing in the streams; played pool, ping-pong, and video games in the rec center at the base; and had sleepovers night after night without having to get permission from our parents. Those were wonderful times. We knew they couldn't last forever—somebody's dad was always being transferred—although it sure felt as if they would.

Now I was in South Carolina, where you were supposed to stick to your own kind. Oh, you might get away with spending time with white kids in your house, or even as you waited together at the bus stop, but the moment you could be seen by the rest of the kids at school, you were expected to choose sides. Never was the gap more apparent than in the cafeteria at lunchtime. The whites sat with the whites, the blacks with the blacks. You'd swear it was 1958, not 1988.

On my first day at Ebenezer, which was mostly black, I was walking by this one white kid when I heard him say, "Bo." I kept walking. *He can't be talking to me,* I thought.

He was, and he would not be the only white kid to call me that. Over time, I became resigned to hearing it and even convinced myself it was a sign of being accepted, sort of like being called "dude."

How naive I was. Bo, I found out, was slang for "Boy." In my opinion, that is almost as degrading as the n-word, and it didn't make any difference that the blacks, as well as the whites, began to call me Bo. Because as much as some blacks might see it as an endearing way to address one another, the connotation of the word, said by a master to his slave, makes it too offensive to ever be used. I mentioned it to my father, who told me some guy at the base also called him Bo. It provided some comfort, I suppose, that I wasn't the only one.

No matter. Bo it was, and there wasn't anything I could do about it. What was in my control was whether I would choose the black kids or the white kids when the bus pulled up each morning to the front door of Ebenezer.

I chose a third option: basketball. And whoever showed up to play with me—they could've been yellow or green, for all I cared—that's who I'd be friends with.

I first fell in love with basketball when I was eight years old and we were living in Saxmundham, a town near Bentwaters Royal Air Force Base in England.

My parents played on semipro teams in the area that did quite well. Dad could shoot it from anywhere, with his left or right hand, while Mom, I kid you not, went by the nickname of "Truck." She was like a bulldozer the way she ran over people, and she never hesitated to throw an elbow or two. Mom, whose real name was Flora—everyone called her Flo—could score and rebound. I played for a few teams later on that could have used her.

While people in the crowd were cheering them on, my attention was spent looking underneath the stands for change that might have fallen from anybody's pockets. You'd be surprised how much I could collect in a couple of hours.

After one game, however, with my parents in the locker room and no one else around, I picked up a basketball for the first time and took a few shots. Then—and I don't know what compelled me—I came up with a drill: three layups from the left side of the basket with my left hand, and three from the right side with my right hand. To complete the drill successfully, I had to make six layups without a miss. Nothing to it, I figured. Mom and Dad made shooting layups look easy.

Not for me, I failed.

I did what I usually did when events didn't go my way. I started to cry. I could not understand why I didn't make every shot. Not once did I consider that the baskets were 10 feet high and I was around half that size.

I didn't pick up a ball again our entire time in England, though it had nothing to do with the missed layups. I was busy with other activities, and there was no playground or court close to our apartment. Not until about two years later did I give the game another chance. I joined a league at Edwards for sixth- and seventh-graders, and it wasn't long before I figured out I was pretty good. Whenever I threw the ball in the vicinity of the hoop, more often than not it went in.

My form was not a sight to behold. I would cross my arms, tuck the ball under my chin, and let it go with two hands, all while jumping toward the basket. Yikes. How the ball ever dropped through the net is beyond me. Jeff Lensch, one of my coaches, took on the challenge of correcting these flaws.

Brave man. He shot video of me, and watching the footage helped immensely. His advice was simple:

Jump straight up. Bring your elbows in. Put one hand under the ball, the other on the side. Point your toes at the basket. Bend your knees. And keep your eyes on the rim the whole time.

Jeff took me to my first NBA game. It was in March 1987, and the Los Angeles Lakers were hosting the Detroit Pistons at the Fabulous Forum, as it was known.

As we watched the players warm up on opposite sides of the court, I couldn't get over how tall the two starting centers were. The Lakers' legendary Kareem Abdul-Jabbar and the Pistons' Bill Laimbeer sure did not look that tall on TV.

Jeff said he'd give me $20 if I could get Kareem's autograph. Way to go out on a limb. I had as good a chance of blocking one of Kareem's famous sky hooks. Besides, I was a shy boy, and after seeing others get turned down, I didn't even ask. I also noticed Kareem was in the middle of his routine and sensed this was a sacred time for a player in the NBA. Man, was I right about that. In those days, I was too young to grasp the nuances of the game, but I knew there was more to it than making shots.

Which might explain why my favorite Laker in the Showtime Era of the 1980s wasn't Kareem or Magic Johnson or the speedy James Worthy. My favorite Laker was not even one of the starting five. It was Michael Cooper, a thin, six-foot-five guard, who did the things you need to win basketball games, the things that don't show up on *SportsCenter*:

Box out your man. Deflect a pass. Set a pick. Take a charge.

That was Coop, night after night.

Jeff, along with Phil Pleasant, another coach, drilled me on the fundamentals until the ball wasn't the only thing that was spinning:

How to dribble on my left side.

How to shoot layups with my right hand.

How to throw a bounce pass.

How to make a sharp cut.

How to give a pump fake.

No part of the game was overlooked. I was so focused on learning the fundamentals that, to this day, I can't be sure who was the head coach, Jeff or Phil. Either way, when I found out we were moving to South Carolina, besides having to leave friends yet again, I worried I'd never find coaches as devoted and knowledgeable as these two were.

How backward those outdoor courts at Ebenezer, with their chain rims and gravel pavement, seemed then. How beautiful they seem now.

We had about 20 minutes before school began, enough time to squeeze in a game or two. They played a different brand of basketball in South Carolina, I soon discovered, than what I was used to in California. They raced down the court and used their athletic skills instead of relying on pump fakes, setting screens, and cutting to the hoop. There was also more pushing and scratching and clawing.

And fighting. The big kids were so intimidating—some already had full-grown beards—that no one would dare to challenge them. It was the smaller kids you had to watch out for. Being constantly shoved around, they felt the need to prove how tough they were.

The bell rang at 8:30, and everyone hurried to class. The game, however, was on my mind all the time. It might sound corny, but I was getting to know the ball:

How some spin one way, and others another.

How to aim for a higher arc when you shoot.

How to dribble so you didn't lose the handle.

There was little about the ball I wasn't getting to know. This was important because the ball is the one part of the game that you *can* control. You can't control the opponent or your teammates. Only the ball will be there for you. As long as you are there for the ball.

Over time, as I won one game after another, kids came by to watch me play. That was exciting, and not just because of how much I loved to compete. Basketball was my way to get them to accept me and stop claiming I talked like a white kid.

One day, for some reason, I began to throw up these wild sky hooks from every part of the court. It so happened that the captain of the football team and one of his friends were watching when I swished one from about 20 feet. Total luck. And what timing!

"This kid can play," the captain said.

For the most part, I played the way the other kids played—pushing the ball, taking a quick shot, being in a track meet as much as a basketball game. Though I never forgot the fundamentals I learned in California. They would serve me well for a long time.

Only, performing well on the playground wouldn't be good enough. I would have to perform well in games that counted, and I would soon get my chance.

The announcement came over the loudspeaker:

"Anyone who is trying out for the basketball team, be in the gym tomorrow before school starts."

I showed up, of course, but so did a lot of other kids, and nothing was guaranteed. The coach divided us into groups of three and told everybody to shoot 25 free throws. I was a pretty decent free-throw shooter, remembering to bend my knees and keep my eyes on the rim, as my coaches in California taught me, but what if I had an off day? Would my basketball career be over before it started?

Fortunately, I didn't. I made 23 of the 25, far more than anyone else, and I could tell the coach was impressed. Can't say the same for this other boy, Kenny—not his real name— who was trying out.

"You won't make the team," Kenny told me.

I didn't say a word. What *do* you say to someone like that, someone who doesn't know anything about you? Why he was so negative, to this day, I have no idea.

A few days after the tryout, when I found out that, yes, I had made the team, Kenny tried again to bring me down.

"That doesn't mean anything," he said. "You won't start!"

Again, I didn't say a word.

He wasn't a bad person, and besides, we've all had a Kenny or two in our lives, someone who tells us we're not good enough. The question is: Do we let ourselves believe them?

If anything, I'm glad Kenny said what he did, and when he said it. His voice stayed in my head for a long time, propelling me forward when I had doubts, and there were many. *I'll start, Kenny, you'll see, and I'll be one of the best players on the team!* He was the first to motivate me by being critical, but he wouldn't be the last.

Making the team paid off big-time. Many of those who saw me as an outsider now thought I was cool. Better yet, I wasn't judged as belonging to one group or the other.

"He plays basketball, he's an athlete," they said, instead of, "He hangs out with the white kids."

Another benefit was that, on game days, I was allowed to wear my warm-up suit to school, which gave me a third outfit to go along with the two pairs of jeans. As I walked down those halls, I felt a sense of pride I'd never felt before.

A few kids even started to think there was something special about me, and it wasn't only because of my basketball skills.

One day a bunch of us were in the locker room waiting for practice to begin. I don't remember what got into me, but I bragged to everyone that I knew how to pick locks. Sure you do, they said, blowing me off. Fine, I will show you, I told them. I went up to a random locker, spun the lock around two or three times, put my ear against it, as they do in the movies, and, would you believe it, the darn thing opened! It was almost as if God himself decided he was going to do a favor for me.

"How did you do that?" they wanted to know. "Do another," they pleaded.

Nope. One was enough, knowing I could never be that lucky again.

Strange as it may seem, picking the lock was a big deal. Kids that age are always looking for a way to impress the others in their group.

When it came to basketball, though, I didn't have to

count on luck. I got better and better from hard work, nothing else. Come the fall of 1990, I would be headed to Hillcrest, where the crowds were larger and the stakes greater.

I hoped I was up to it.

3

HIGH SCHOOL AND HIGH HOPES

I was up to the challenge, all right, and not just because of the work I put in on the playground and on the junior high team, but because of Saturday and Sunday mornings at Shaw Air Force Base, where Dad worked.

On those mornings, he and others on the base got together for a few friendly games of hoop. Okay, maybe not so friendly; man, those guys took it seriously. They would show up at 9:30, sometimes earlier, to write their names on the board for five-on-five, full-court games that began at 10:00. Get there much later, and you ran the risk of waiting a long time to play or not playing at all.

My dad wasn't the waiting type. He would leave for

Shaw promptly at 9, and if I was not ready to go, I got left behind. We had a carport underneath the house, so I could hear that old Trans van of his starting up while I was still in bed. I'd grab my sneakers and pick up something good for breakfast to make it downstairs in time, and if I was too late, I hopped on my bike or called a friend to give me a ride. I wouldn't miss those games for anything.

Although, according to several members of the gym staff, I shouldn't have been there in the first place. The others who played were in their twenties and thirties, a few in their forties. I was 13, and the concern was that I was taking up a spot that belonged to men who worked there.

It was a good thing that, as time went on, I began to look a lot older than my age—I grew five inches between eighth and ninth grades, to six-foot-two—so Dad slipped me in, and no one had a problem. Except for the time someone on the gym staff stopped us at the front door. Dad pointed out I'd been coming to the games for well over a year and was better than players twice my age. Taller too. Even so, the man wouldn't budge, and not surprisingly, Dad caused a little scene and was cited for insubordination.

I wasn't embarrassed in the least. I was proud. My father had stood up for me.

Dad, you see, wasn't overly affectionate toward me, or any of my siblings, nor did he play with me around the house. Legos, toys, football, nothing. I don't remember any one-on-one time, come to think of it, and I'm pretty sure it was the same between him and the others. Not once did he tell me, "I love you," and looking back, I wish he had. It might have made me more comfortable saying "I love you" to them, or anybody I've felt close to.

Still, I was always aware that he loved us as much as he was capable of loving, and that morning at Shaw was just one way he showed it.

I learned a lot playing ball there, and it went well beyond the game itself. It spoke to the fundamental difference between success and failure. The men had done extremely well in their lives, supporting their families and serving their country, but maybe there had been a wrong decision, or two, earlier that kept them from attaining their true dream: to be a professional athlete. I can't tell you how many complained to me that they would have made it if not for the alcohol and the women and the other mistakes of youth, and how they'd do it differently if they could start over. I believed them. They were that good.

That won't be me, I told myself. *I won't be sharing my regrets with a kid 20 years from now at some military base on a Saturday morning. I won't envy the promise he has, because I'm not going to throw away my own.*

The games themselves went quickly, the winners being the first team to reach 11 points. They then took on the next team on the list, while the losers fell to the bottom, which was the worst feeling you could imagine. You'd kill time by shooting at another basket in the gym or lifting weights, but even if you got to play again—and there was no guarantee— you'd face a team that was exhausted. Beating them wouldn't prove anything.

The action could get quite physical, but with no officials, you had to call your own fouls, and people, by and large, didn't say anything unless it was clear they were hacked.

"Respect my call," they'd say.

Of course, similar to pickup games throughout America,

there was always that one guy who cried "foul!" whenever he missed a shot. Heck, I knew players in the NBA who looked for a referee every time they didn't score.

"You hit my hand," they'd complain.

So what? That's not a foul. The hand is a part of the ball. You'd be amazed how many players don't know that. The fact was, they missed the shot. Everyone misses shots.

I won my share of games at Shaw, thanks to my dad, who was one of the top shooters, and my brother, John, the football star. Other guys, whenever they saw us coming, used to say: "Uh-oh, the Allens just walked in." They called us "Showtime," after the legendary Lakers teams. We took the ball, ran down the floor, and put it in the basket. One possession after another.

I also lost my share. The top players in the area showed up, and believe me, they came to play. Some had trouble getting in at first, but a lot of times we would meet at the front gate and make sure somebody sponsored them. We, the Allens, wanted to be the best. In order to do that, we had to beat the best.

Before I played at Shaw, I knew how to shoot, but I didn't know how to dunk. I wasn't tall enough to try. Shaw was where I learned, and one dunk in particular was more memorable than the others.

It happened on one of the days I was too late to catch a ride with Dad. A friend and I wrote our names on the board, and we wound up playing against my father, who was feeling good about himself after winning a few games. I don't recall what the score was, but I was on a fast break when a teammate passed the ball to me in the lane. Who was the only person between me and the basket? You guessed it. I went up as high as I could and . . . *slam!*

Everyone in the gym went crazy.

"He dunked on his dad!" they screamed. "He dunked on his dad!"

The dunk didn't mean very much to me at the time—it was only one point and we still had a game to win—but soon after it meant quite a bit. It meant I had reached a new level as a player, and I'd only get better. When you can dunk, it's like you are playing on the fifth floor while everybody else is stuck on the first. There's nothing in basketball as demoralizing. The players you dunk on know there is little they can do to stop you.

Dad, however, didn't say a word about the dunk, not then, or ever, so I can't be sure how he felt. Like I said, we didn't have that kind of relationship. He didn't offer compliments or encouragement; that was Mom's job. She was the person, from day one, who said I'd be the best player in the world.

Hillcrest High was also in the middle of nowhere, although because it was just off Highway 441 and you didn't enter via a dirt road, you felt a little closer to civilization. And the water in the fountains, thank goodness, didn't come out orange at first.

The school wasn't very big, about 200 students per class, but big enough to be a part of Class 4A, which meant I would go against the better players in the state. I needed that type of challenge to have any chance of receiving a college scholarship.

I also needed to watch myself off the court. I saw kids routinely pull out wads of twenties in the cafeteria, and I was pretty sure how they made that money. Yet I wasn't tempted in the least by the whole drug scene. I have never even held a joint in my hand, and that includes the years in college and the NBA.

Needless to say, one can still be in the wrong place at the wrong time, which scared the heck out of my mother. My curfew was 12:00 AM, and there was no room for negotiating. She would have been one tough GM.

"You don't need to put yourself in compromising situations," she told me. "You are going to get out of here. You are going to do something good with your life."

She knew what she was talking about. Take what happened to a good friend of mine:

He went to a club one Friday evening and ended up killing someone. I could have easily been with him and either ended up in jail, as he did, as an accomplice or, God forbid, been shot myself. Such was the world I was living in. Which was why I was more than content to stay home with my brother and sisters while everybody else was out at all hours of the night.

Not going to the parties or the dances at school set me further apart socially, but it was a price I was willing to pay. Besides, getting to bed early made it easy for me to be the first one at the gym the following morning, and nothing was more important.

At the same time, I wasn't exactly a monk. I was a man. With certain needs, if you know what I mean.

Her name was Rosalind, and we could not have had less in common. She was a senior; I was a sophomore. She was part of the "in" group; I wasn't part of any group. She'd had boyfriends before; I'd never been in a relationship.

What we did have in common was being tall—she was six-foot—and slim, and we were both virgins. Every night since I was about 14 I'd gone to sleep wondering: *When am I going to get laid?* It could not happen soon enough. Remember, I hung around kids who were having sex before they were learning how to drive. I had not even been to first base!

So when a friend told me about a gorgeous girl with short, dark hair who had just broken up with her boyfriend and was asking about me . . . *me* . . . I made my move. I don't recall what I said, but knowing how shy I was around girls, I'm sure it couldn't have been very smooth.

Whatever it was, it worked. Rosalind and I exchanged numbers, and before long we were an item, though it took a while for her to trust that this was going to last. Day after day, I'd follow her down the hall, but she'd always walk a couple of steps in front and never wait for me to catch up. Whether it had to do with the difference in our status in school, I couldn't be certain, but I didn't have the nerve to ask her to slow down. I also didn't have the nerve to be more passionate, and she wasn't pleased. I'd give her a peck on the cheek, but that was about it.

"We should be kissing to the point where I don't have any lipstick on by the time we're done," she told a friend of ours. One day, finally, I kissed her like she wanted to be kissed, and she didn't complain ever again.

By junior year, whenever Rosalind made the short trip home from Columbia, where she attended college, we'd hang out at my house or hers.

You can guess what happened next. And when she got pregnant, there was not any doubt we'd keep the baby. Nor was there any doubt we'd get married. That was simply what one did in the South in the early 1990s, and truth is, I was looking forward to it. Rosalind and I loved each other. Why not share our love with a child?

I would still have to get through high school, and then, hopefully, college. No one in my family had earned a college degree, and that meant more to my mom than anything. Take care of your education, she assured me, and she would help take care of the baby.

Still, I was terrified. Who in my situation wouldn't be? The day would come, and soon, when that child would be my responsibility, and I knew nothing about being a father or raising a family. I was critical of some of the choices my father made, but I hadn't been dealing with the pressures he faced. Perhaps there was a lot more to being the head of a household than I thought.

Helping me cope with these fears, in addition to the assurances from my mother, was the faith I gained from being around the military. I don't presume for a second to have been familiar with what went on in the minds of those who put their lives on the line, but seeing how they handled themselves, I came to realize that, as long as you have a pulse, you should be able to deal with any obstacle. Knowing that I would have a child to support forced me to focus more on my future. It wouldn't be only about me anymore.

My lone regret is that I wasn't there to see the birth of our daughter, Tierra, in the fall of my senior year. I had been told Rosalind was in the hospital for a checkup, not that she was in labor. I was in school when Mom came by to give me the news. When I arrived at the hospital and got a first look at my little girl, I was overcome again with the enormity of the task in front of me.

I saw Tierra almost every day, Rosalind wanting to make sure she became familiar with her daddy before I left for college. During those first weeks, I was as inept as I feared. I could change her diapers and feed her, but not having spent a great deal of time around babies, I didn't know how to simply sit and play with her.

Meanwhile, Mom, as promised, bought the diapers, baby food, milk, and clothing we needed. Given her own finances, this was no small sacrifice.

I first saw the Hillcrest basketball coach, James Smith, while I was in junior high. He was always screaming at his players for one reason or another. One time, I kid you not, I watched him throw a ball rack at them. *This man is crazy*, I thought.

I couldn't have been more wrong. In the three years I played for Coach Smith, he hardly ever raised his voice. In fact, most of the time he was so quiet you didn't know he was there. To me, that is one of the highest compliments you can pay a coach. Same with the refs; we should never know their names. The game, at any level, should be about the players. That's who fans come to see.

Coach Smith made sure we were in the best shape possible. We ran 3.1 miles each day after school. That was when I discovered my love, and hatred, of running.

He registered us in cross-country meets in the area, and though we normally got dusted, we were slowly getting used to what it felt like to dig deep within ourselves. In practice,

I would occasionally look over at him when he'd blow the whistle to have us run a few laps and think: *Is he blind? Doesn't he get it that we have nothing left?* But we did have something left, and he knew it.

We weren't one of the best teams in the state. Not yet. We were still learning how to play with one another, and that takes time. Several of us had been on the same team for two years at Ebenezer, but the competition in high school was much fiercer. The biggest accomplishment in my sophomore year was knocking off our main rival, Sumter High. We felt like we had won the state championship. I averaged 20.5 points and 10 rebounds that season, but I wasn't aggressive or aware enough of the entire court. That would come later.

Meanwhile, being on the team did even more for my image than it did in junior high. Few kids came to the games at Ebenezer, so they usually found out what happened through an announcement over the loudspeaker: "The ninth-grade boys beat so-and-so, Ray Allen leading the way with 12 points." At Hillcrest, the results were published in the newspaper. A lot of my classmates wanted to be seen with me, and as I became known as a jock, I was once more able to avoid the no-win choice between the whites and the blacks.

On the other hand, no matter how much I achieved on the court, and whatever status I helped lend the school, some kids still wouldn't accept me, and that would always be the case. I wasn't one of them, and by "them," I mean those who had spent their entire lives in Dalzell.

I'll give you a perfect illustration. The whole senior class met in the cafeteria to hand out the awards they give at probably every high school in America—you know, Class Clown, Best Couple, Most Likely to Be President, etc.

One by one, each student who was named went up to the front to receive a certificate, everybody applauding. But when they called my name, for being the Most Likely to Succeed, the room went dead silent. Considering how well I had played that year, they thought they had no choice but to give me the honor, but that didn't mean they were happy about it. I almost felt like I was doing something wrong by accepting it.

People, my teammates included, were always waiting for me to do or say the wrong thing, and when I did, they took advantage. Such as the interview I gave in the cafeteria with a local TV station after I won the state Player of the Week award. Instead of using the word "gym," I referred to it as a gymnasium. They got a big chuckle out of that. No one in Dalzell would ever use the word "gymnasium."

Or the time, in a game senior year against West Florence, when I grabbed the ball on the opening tip and scored on a reverse tomahawk dunk. All I heard was silence in return. *Why aren't the fans going nuts? You can't tell me that wasn't one of the more spectacular dunks you have ever seen.*

"That wasn't our basket," a teammate said.

Oops. I was embarrassed, to say the least, and although it made no difference in the outcome—we killed them—I had a feeling I'd hear about that dunk for a long time. I wouldn't be shocked if some of my former teammates still tell the story.

Many of them would come over to the house and we'd hang out for a while, but I always sensed a barrier between us, and it wasn't merely because I didn't come from their world. It was also because of my success, and them understanding, as my mother said, that I would get out of there and do something good with my life, and they most likely would not. One teammate fouled me so hard on purpose in practice that I got scratches everywhere and was bleeding. Another told people that I might receive a college scholarship, but I'd sit on the bench for four years and come back to town an alcoholic. It reminded me of Kenny, the kid from junior high, who said I would never make the team.

It got to the point where I stopped sharing good news, even with those I had assumed cared about me. When my teammate Chris (not his real name), failed to say a word any time I showed him a recruiting letter I received, I realized it was because the letters from colleges were pouring in for me but not for him. I decided not to show him, or anyone, another letter. Chris would wind up going to a small university in South Carolina, and we'd lose touch. Moral of the story: Don't get too excited about your success in front of others. Many don't care if you succeed, and quite a few hope you'll fail.

Besides, I couldn't waste time on what others might think of me. There was too much work to do. In the summer between 10th and 11th grades, I competed in AAU (Amateur Athletic Union) ball against a number of the top players in Washington, DC, and Virginia. DC, in those days, was the crossover capital of high school basketball; I had never seen such crazy handles with the ball anywhere. The best part of AAU was getting a chance to play in big cities and to meet kids from all over South Carolina, including one from Greenville, about 150 miles northwest of Dalzell.

The kid was Kevin Garnett.

Kevin and I had a mutual friend who picked me up first, then him, and drove us to Columbia to play against guys from the University of South Carolina. The trip took a couple of hours, but that's what you do if you're 16 years old and you want to find out how you match up against players older than you. The two of us got to know each other quite well that summer.

"Man, you're like Jordan," Kevin used to say. "Every time he scores 30, you score 35."

Believe me, I was no Jordan, but I was clearly a better player my junior year, and the summer in AAU ball was one of the reasons. I found the aggression I didn't have in my sophomore year, and it also had to do with how assertive I had become in my relationship with Rosalind. I was gaining confidence by the day.

Our team was also getting better. We knew which plays worked and which ones didn't. Coach Smith let us play. He said less than ever.

He was also a huge help with the recruiting letters. Some coaches, when they have a player who is attracting attention from top schools, see the situation as an opportunity—for *themselves*, not just the kid.

You want him to play for you, fine, you have to take me too.

Conversely, if a school doesn't take the coach, the implication is: *I'll make sure the kid goes somewhere else.*

That wasn't Coach Smith. Did he want to advance in his career? You bet. Except he would advance the right way, and not exploit me, or anyone, as a bargaining chip. I was so naive, it wasn't until years later, when I was a pro, that I learned about the deals recruiters routinely made, as they say, under the table: offering cars, women, cash, you name it. No one offered me a dime, and that's probably because they didn't believe I was good enough. The Class of 1993 included players a lot more heralded than I was, such as Rasheed Wallace, Jerry Stackhouse, and Jeff McInnis, all of whom would one day play in the NBA.

There were times I, too, wondered if I was good enough, like in the summer after 11th grade when I attended the annual Nike camp in Indianapolis. Seeing a gap between the other players and myself, I realized I couldn't just beat the competition back in South Carolina; I had to dominate. It really hit me when I wasn't selected for the All-Star Game near the end of camp. Which, I should add, was to be shown on television.

I watched the game from the bleachers next to Stephon Marbury, who was only going into 10th grade.

"Yo," Stephon said. "I saw you play all week. You're better than they are."

"What am I supposed to do?" I told him. "Run down to the floor and tell them to put me in?"

From the look on his face, that's exactly what he thought I should do. Little could either of us have imagined that, in four years' time, he and I would be back-to-back picks in the NBA Draft, and be traded for each other the same night. We hadn't made it to college yet.

I left Indianapolis more dedicated than ever. As a senior, I was the Gatorade Player of the Year in South Carolina, averaging 28.5 points, 13 rebounds, and six assists. I even was given a nickname, "Candy Man," from a coach who was also the public-address announcer.

"Everything you do is so sweet," he told me.

Word traveled fast, especially in a small state like ours. Since our gym seated about only 650, people would squeeze in the side door and stand up the whole time. They came to find out for themselves if I was as good as they had been told. First, they had to find out who I was, period. This was years before the Internet, where your face is everywhere. I'd be warming up before a game when I'd overhear fans searching for me:

"That's him over there."

"No, it's not. That other guy is Ray Allen."

"You're wrong. He's the one by the free-throw line."

I preferred to have the attention on the team, not on me. We deserved it. By this point, we were among the finest in the state.

Besides playing together since eighth grade, some of my teammates and I competed in the games at Shaw and on courts near my house. As we got taller—I was now six-five, while the others were six-three or six-two—we learned to play above the rim, practicing at first with a volleyball, which we could palm, before moving on to the real thing. Every so often we'd face a team with a player who was six-eight or six-nine, but it was never anybody who could take over a game.

We were simply more athletic than everybody else. In one of our set plays, I'd throw the ball to Ronnie Morant, who we called "T," on the block, and dart down the lane. He'd toss it high in the air, and I'd slam it home. The other team knew what was coming but couldn't stop it.

Sometimes teams didn't know what was coming. We had this one trick play where it appeared that T would be the in-bounds passer, but as soon as the ref handed him the ball, I'd say loud enough for the guy guarding me to hear: "I'm supposed to take the ball out." The defender would relax, for an instant, and that was all I needed. T would hit me as I cut to the hoop for an easy dunk.

We went 23-4 during the regular season and kept the momentum going in the playoffs, which were held at Morris College in Sumter. In the state championship game against James F. Byrnes on the University of South Carolina campus, we grabbed a 40–14 lead in the first half, and began to celebrate. Prematurely.

With only a few minutes to go, the lead was down to single digits. To this day, I don't know how they came back. Fortunately, I nailed a couple of jumpers and made a dunk to seal it for us. I finished with 25 points and 15 rebounds. We were the state champions!

One would think winning the title would make us heroes in Dalzell, then and forever. Not so. No parade, no keys to the city, nothing. That said everything one needed to know about the differences between high school basketball and football in the South. Win the state in football, you're a legend. Basketball took such a backseat that we had to take up collections to buy uniforms and shoes and to go on road trips.

Yet I wasn't bitter. If anything, I was grateful for my years in South Carolina—grateful for discovering the courage I wasn't sure I had and, of course, for the woman I fell in love with and the girl we were raising together.

In California, I could do little wrong, but in South Carolina, I came to realize there would always be people testing me, and the question was: Would I become what some hoped I would be, a failure, or what I hoped to be—a winner, on and off the court? That's the challenge facing all of us: to overcome the doubts others have about us and the doubts we ourselves have.

I changed in South Carolina for good. And for the better.

4

GO NORTH, YOUNG MAN

The first letters came junior year from small schools mostly in the South: Furman, Liberty, Mercer, Winthrop, East Carolina, Campbell University, UNC-Charlotte, and East Tennessee State.

I was thrilled to open every one of them, no matter the size or prestige of the school. Barring any mishaps during my senior year at Hillcrest, I would be going to college, and that was something I never took for granted. Most of the kids I played with in high school would have given anything for one letter. From anywhere.

Going to college would also mean I could think of a career in the NBA. Sure, the idea had been in the back of my mind for years, ever since the day I saw Michael Jordan on TV against the Knicks, but it seemed closer to fantasy than reality. Think about it: No one from Dalzell, South Carolina, had ever made it to the NBA. Why would I, Walter Ray Allen Jr., the son of an Air Force technician, be any different?

I had been too busy, in any case, with each step along the way to get ahead of myself. I have long believed that if you focus too much on the next level, you will not succeed at the current level. Give your very best in the situation you're in, and the rest will take care of itself.

Of the schools I heard from, I was most intrigued by UNC-Charlotte, the 49ers, who seemed more interested in me than the others were. So what if it wasn't a top-tier program? The 49ers competed against a lot of quality teams, which would give me the exposure I was looking for, and there was no reason, if I performed well enough, I couldn't go from there to the NBA. That's what Cedric Maxwell, who played for the Boston Celtics in the 1970s and '80s, did.

I also liked the city. Charlotte was far enough away, roughly 100 miles, that I would feel I was on my own, yet close enough for friends and family to visit. I could definitely see myself going there.

Besides, I did not expect to hear from the bigger colleges. No one in Dalzell did. In football, yes. Basketball, never.

I was wrong.

Not long afterward, I heard from one major school after another: Wake Forest. Virginia. Southern Cal. Villanova. And so on. Then I was really excited. I put each letter in a large treasure chest that belonged to my dad. The chest was a time capsule for me. I knew, even then, there would be a lot of ups and downs through the years, but whatever happened, I would always have the chest to remind me of this special time in my life.

There were occasions, I must admit, when it was overwhelming. Wake Forest sent me a letter almost every day, and not just about their basketball team. They sent articles about other teams to show that I would be a part of the entire university community. After a while, I stopped reading them.

Some letters seemed to have been written by someone who had attended one of my games; the details were specific and the sentiments personal. Others felt like they'd been written by a secretary in a coach's office, who wouldn't be able to tell the difference between Ray Allen and Ray Alston. It reminds me of the guys, and you know the type, who hit on a dozen different girls at the same time. One is bound to go out with them.

I've forgotten some of the schools that wrote, or called, but there is one call I will never forget.

"You're a hell of a player," Dean Smith said.

Yes, Dean Smith, the coach at North Carolina. No figure in the sport was more revered than he was.

"I want you to know I think you'll have a great career," he went on. "We're not recruiting you, because we have someone on our roster at your position. If we didn't, we would definitely be interested in you. I wish you the best of luck."

If that wasn't the epitome of class, I don't know what is. And he didn't need me. The "someone" Coach Smith was referring to was Jerry Stackhouse, who would go on to be a star for the Tar Heels.

Come senior year, the clock was ticking and I had to narrow my choices down to five. That is the maximum number of official visits the NCAA allows you to make, and I was not going to commit myself to four years at a place I never saw in person.

Two schools I hoped to put in the final five were Clemson and UCLA. I fell in love with Clemson when I went to a basketball camp there one summer, and I was a Bruins fan during our years in California. With the ten national championships won by John Wooden in the 1960s and '70s, no program was more successful than theirs. As a kid, I walked everywhere wearing a blue-and-gold Bruins hat and jersey.

Neither made the list.

Clemson was out because the Tigers were likely to go on probation, and I couldn't take a risk. UCLA was out because the Bruins apparently weren't in need of my services. I never heard a word from them.

Early on, another possibility was Virginia. I was impressed by the coach, Jeff Jones, who wanted to play an up-tempo style, and the school was a member of the Atlantic Coast Conference, which had North Carolina and Duke. You can't get better exposure than the ACC. One day, though, out of nowhere, I received a letter stating that the Cavs were no longer recruiting me, as they had signed somebody else with a similar skill set.

A place I didn't consider was the University of South Carolina. No doubt I would have given it serious thought, but like UCLA, there were no letters or phone calls, which was surprising, since I was one of the best players in the state. Not until months later did the coaches reach out, and that was only because the school had failed to bring on other players it was recruiting and was under pressure from the local press.

Too late. I had made up my mind. The final five were

Alabama, Wake Forest, North Carolina State, Kentucky, and the University of Connecticut.

During my junior year, before I settled on those five, one coach after another came to our house, saying all the right things to Mom and me. Dad was in Korea. She didn't pretend to know everything about the game of basketball or the world of academia, but she knew how to listen and ask good questions, and that was just as important.

Dad offered his opinion on the phone, but there was little he could do that far away. You need to determine how sincere the coaches are, and the best way was to look them in the eye. They are no different from any traveling salesman.

Do I wish that Dad could have been more involved in the recruiting process from start to finish? Absolutely. What teenage boy wouldn't want his father to help him make such a potentially life-defining choice? At the same time, because I was often on my own, I'd learned to be independent and trust my instincts. They rarely let me down.

Fortunately, in addition to Coach Smith, one of the football coaches at Hillcrest offered some advice.

"Where do you think I should go to college?" I asked him.

"I would never tell you where to go," he responded.

That's different, I told myself. No one had hesitated to tell me before, and they knew a heck of a lot less about college than the football coach did.

Then came the message that resonated:

"Whatever you do," he said, "make sure that *you* make the decision."

I know it seems obvious, but too many kids allow somebody else—a parent, girlfriend, agent, coach, etc., anybody except themselves—to make the decision.

Listen to those close to you, I tell kids these days. They might see something you don't. Yet always keep in mind that their goals are not necessarily the same as yours. You're the one who will go to classes and take exams. You're the one who must get along with your coaches and teammates. You're the one who will earn a degree, or won't. And you're the one who will look back with pride or regret. I saw some phenomenal players in high school who should have been stars in college, and maybe in the NBA. But they chose what turned out to be the wrong school for them and weren't heard from again.

In October 1992, a week after Tierra was born, I made my first visit, to the University of Alabama. I spent two days in Tuscaloosa, and they were two of the best days I can remember.

One of my hosts was Marvin Orange, a freshman point guard from Irmo High School in the Columbia area, who had been the best player in the state. I didn't know Marvin, though I knew a lot about him. Seeing somebody from my part of the world fit in as well as he did, I thought Alabama could very well be the place for me.

On my first night, I went to a Step Show, where members of different fraternities and sororities use organized step routines, mixed with incredible hip-hop beats, to compete against each other. It suddenly dawned on me: this was what I'd been dreaming about since I was 12 and saw *School Daze*, the movie about students at a black college. They were having a blast, and I couldn't wait to join them.

The following day, I went to a football game. Of course I did. On no campus in America was football perhaps bigger than at Alabama, where the coach for many years, Paul

William "Bear" Bryant, was more well-known than the governor—and the pope as well. The Crimson Tide, as usual, rolled over South Carolina, 48–7.

Yet, as much fun as I was having, two things happened during my visit that made me question whether Alabama was the place for me after all.

One incident occurred before lunch in Birmingham on the day I arrived. We stopped there to meet another recruit before going to campus. I got out of the car and was walking toward the restaurant when I made eye contact with the driver of a pickup truck. He stuck out his middle finger. *He can't possibly be mad at me,* I told myself. *I didn't do anything wrong.*

I didn't have to do anything wrong. I was black, he was white, and we were in Alabama. That was wrong enough. I went inside, had a nice lunch, and didn't tell anyone. I didn't see the point. There was nothing another player or a coach could have done about the guy in the truck. I'd have to decide for myself if I could live with that amount of racism around me. Because it wasn't about to go away.

The other incident took place at the football game. As a prized recruit, I figured I'd get a decent seat, perhaps close to the 50-yard line. I didn't get any seat at all. I was forced to stand in the aisle the whole time. The basketball coaches didn't have a lot of clout or they didn't think I was important enough. Either way, I was concerned I'd be going to a school where, once again, basketball ranked far below football.

Still, I didn't take Alabama out of the running. As a matter of fact . . .

"You had a great time, didn't you?" said Gregg Polinsky, an assistant coach, before I headed back to South Carolina.

"Yes, I had a great time," I admitted.

"Alabama is the only place for you," Coach Polinsky added.

Then, using what he knew about my situation at home, he made his closing argument. He was clearly a pro at this.

"You have to start making mature decisions," he told me. "You've got a daughter to take care of. You have to tell me you want to come here."

I don't have to tell him a thing, I thought.

Yet he kept going on and on about why I had to choose Alabama. Finally, I gave in. I committed. I didn't want to let him down.

Not surprisingly, the moment I got back to Dalzell, people told me I was crazy for making such a rash decision. The football coach who had given me great advice before put it best:

"You may love Alabama, and in the end that very well might be the best place for you," he said. "But how are you going to know unless you see what else is out there?"

I knew he was right before he finished his sentence. I had four more visits I could make, and that was what I would do. Forget about not wanting to let down the Alabama coach. This was my future, not his.

He didn't take it well. I felt he'd been trying to manipulate me by saying how mature I needed to be to raise my child. Now he told me how *immature* I was because I had the nerve to visit other colleges. He also mentioned there was somebody else Alabama was recruiting, and if he signed—he later did—there would not be a spot for me.

Nice try. It didn't work.

"This is what I have to do," I told Coach Polinsky. "If that's who you want, do what you have to do."

I shouldn't be too critical. The man was trying to succeed in an intensely competitive business, and when you consider the sleazy way some recruiters behave, his tactics were pretty mild.

I agreed to one compromise: I would visit only two of the four schools, Kentucky and Connecticut. It was a mistake, I know, but it showed again how young and vulnerable I was.

The University of Connecticut was next. Connecticut? What would ever possess me to put that school in the final five?

A big-name coach? Nope.

A big-time tradition? Not exactly.

A big-city environment? Please.

What then?

Decency, integrity, honesty.

I remember the first time I heard from them. On the phone was Howie Dickenman, one of their assistant coaches, who had watched me at an AAU tournament in Jacksonville. That day, he put a "P" next to my name. "P," short for potential.

"I'm from UConn," Coach Dickenman told me during the call. "I'm very interested in recruiting you."

I was confused.

"UConn? Wait a minute, isn't that near Alaska?" I said.

I'm not kidding. I thought he was calling from the Yukon territory. I didn't know they played basketball up there!

After we got a chuckle out of that, the coach and I enjoyed a wonderful chat. I don't recall exactly what he said, but there was something about his raspy northeastern accent that made me feel comfortable. He and the other Connecticut coaches, I could tell, didn't believe in BS. How refreshing. I'd heard enough already from other recruiters. At Alabama, for example, they said I would go from there right to the NBA. I appreciated their faith in me, but no one is guaranteed a future at the next level.

The UConn coaches, on the other hand, said nothing about the NBA. They didn't even make promises about my freshman year.

"We'll give you the opportunity to be as successful as you want," they explained, "but it's up to you how much work you put in."

Those were precisely the words I wanted to hear. It had been up to me to put in the work at Ebenezer, at Shaw, at Hillcrest, in the AAU games. And if I went to UConn and I wasn't successful, at least I would know I'd been given a fair shot. You can't ask for anything more.

After my conversation with Coach Dickenman, I did some research of my own. Before then, I had known little about the school, and what I did know did not make me fond of the place. That's because, in the 1990 NCAA Tournament East Regional Semifinals, UConn defeated my beloved Clemson Tigers on a miracle jump shot by Tate George at the buzzer. I was devastated. Two days later, in the final, UConn lost a heartbreaker of its own, to Duke, Christian Laettner hitting a jumper as time ran out. Justice served, in my opinion.

I could tell it was a program on the rise, even if it had yet to make an appearance in a Final Four, let alone win a national championship. Under Jim Calhoun, who took over as the coach in 1986, the Huskies were 118-73, a more than respectable record, especially in a conference as competitive as the Big East.

Connecticut, as you'd expect, did some research of its own as well. Coach Calhoun came over to our house and watched a game at Hillcrest. Safe to say, it wasn't one of my better performances. I scored just nine points, though it wasn't the other team that held me back; it was my own. Hoping to get noticed themselves, my teammates would not pass the ball to me. Mom was beside herself. Good thing— for them!—she stayed in her seat; her nickname was Truck, in case you forgot. I calmed her down afterward: "Mom, if I'm good, nothing can hold me back."

I knew I'd get more opportunities at tournaments during the summer, and as I said before, there's a lot more to the game than scoring. Coach Calhoun would pay attention to everything I did on the court, and I was confident he'd still want me to join his program.

If only I could decide what I wanted. That would depend on whether I liked the place when I went for my visit.

As it turned out, I loved the place. I loved the state of Connecticut, the town of Storrs, the campus itself, everything.

I showed up on a typically gorgeous fall weekend. On Friday, I sat in on some classes the players attended. I thought that it was so cool they hung out together away from the court. I wasn't as close to some of my teammates in high school. Lots of times, remember, they went out while I was more comfortable staying home.

On Saturday, I attended another football game. Granted, football in Storrs, Connecticut, was nothing like football in Tuscaloosa, Alabama. The Huskies would wind up 5-6 that season. No matter. I had a seat this time, on the 50-yard line no less, and when I got back to South Carolina, I found out that a photo of me at the game had appeared in the local paper in Connecticut. And I hadn't even made my decision yet!

The moment that meant the most to me occurred while

I was in a bar with several of the guys and the song "Wooly Bully" came on. One player, who was black, started to sing along with the white players. I was blown away that he knew the lyrics and that he didn't refuse to listen to the song because it wasn't rap. There didn't seem to be the same racial barrier I was used to in South Carolina. This was the place for me.

Sound familiar? It should. That's exactly what I said after my visit to Alabama, even after the guy gave me the finger, and after I had to stand in the aisle at the football game. I was getting a bit concerned: Was this how I was going to feel after every school I saw?

That's when I knew I had to make the one last visit, to Lexington, Kentucky. As much as I loved Connecticut, I needed to be sure.

Besides, Kentucky was not just any school. Under Adolph Rupp, the Wildcats won four national championships in the 1940s and '50s. Now led by Rick Pitino, another coach making a name for himself, Kentucky was back among the elite just a few years after going on probation for academic and recruiting violations.

I met Coach Pitino earlier that year, when he came to our house. The man knew how to sell himself, and his program, better than anyone. I felt special, wanted. Too bad I didn't feel the same once I got to Lexington. Especially when you consider how I was treated in Storrs.

Two examples stand out:

I was having lunch with the team's star forward, Jamal Mashburn, and his roommate at a restaurant Pitino owned. He happened to be there that afternoon, sitting with some friends a few tables away. Perfect, I figured, he'll stop by for a few minutes to say hello, and I'll learn more to help me make my decision. Only he didn't stop by. He waved, and that was it. Coach Calhoun would never have ignored us. He and I, in fact, enjoyed several meals together on my visit to Storrs.

The second incident took place the next day. I was leaving the dorm and walking to the practice facility when I saw Pitino drive by. He waved again but didn't pull over to chat. I could draw only one conclusion from these two similar situations: go where you are valued, where it's clear somebody wants you to be an essential part of what they're doing. That goes for deciding between colleges or job offers.

No offense to Pitino, but to him I was one of many. If I went to Kentucky, wonderful, he'd find a way to make good use of me, but if not, the program wouldn't suffer one bit. He was accustomed to signing the best high school players in the nation, and that would be true again that year.

In any case, I was sure now: Connecticut it would be.

I can't overstate how excited I was. I'd be playing in the Big East, and I used to love watching those epic battles on TV between Georgetown, Syracuse, Villanova, and St. John's. In my opinion, the Big East, not the ACC or Big Ten, was the best conference. I'd also play in Madison Square Garden in New York City, which wasn't known as the mecca of basketball for nothing.

New York, Philly, Boston—I would see all the big cities, and the big cities would mean big stages and big possibilities. I learned that in the summer between 10th and 11th grades, during the AAU games in DC. If I could hold my own in the Big East, I could set my sights on the NBA, and Coach Calhoun would be the perfect man to prepare me for that move. Look what he did for Reggie Lewis, whom he coached at Northeastern in the mid-1980s. Lewis, may he rest in peace, went on to play six years for the Boston Celtics, which was quite an accomplishment, coming from a college so under the radar.

What's more, in choosing Connecticut, I'd receive the best of both worlds: playing in the city and going to school in the country, away from the distractions that have kept too many young men from reaching their dreams. I thought of my teammate in high school who told people I'd spend four years on the bench and return to Dalzell an alcoholic. I couldn't predict how well I would do at UConn, but he'd be wrong about me.

The Connecticut coaches, from the start, cared about me as a human being, not just as a basketball player. Coach Dickenman made sure he knew the names of my brothers and sisters, and to this day, he sends Tierra a text every year on her birthday. Dave Leitao, another assistant coach, would later open up to me about how much he loved his family. These were grown men who would help me grow.

The decision final, I began to spread the word. For the longest time, no one could believe it.

"Connecticut," they'd say. "Why in the world are you going *there*?"

I couldn't have shocked them any more if I'd said I was going to the moon. I tried to explain my reasoning, but it never seemed to satisfy them.

Months later, when Connecticut fell to Jackson State— *Jackson State!*—90–88 in the first round of the NIT, which is far less prestigious than the NCAA Tournament, they let me have it again.

"Connecticut sucks!" they told me.

"It's going to be different when I get there," I said, and I truly believed it.

My father also couldn't understand why I didn't choose Kentucky, and he expressed his displeasure over the phone from Korea. I wasn't in the mood to hear it.

"You weren't here when Rick Pitino came to the house," I told him. "You don't know what the coaches said or what it felt like to sit in those dorm rooms. Are they going to take care of me? You think I should go to Kentucky for no other reason than it's Kentucky."

Mom wasn't thrilled either. Earlier in the process, she told me: "I don't care where you end up as long as you don't go to Connecticut."

I wasn't angry with her, as I was with my dad. She was a mother who didn't want her son to be far away. At the same time, parents, in my view, must always put what's best for their child first, whether the kid hopes to play in the NBA or be a violinist for the Boston Pops.

Rosalind also didn't want me to be far away. The two of us were as tight as ever. I hope I don't come across too insensitive, but how she felt did not factor into the decision for one second. I needed to do what I believed was the right thing for my future. Besides, in the long run, the better I did wherever I went, the better I could provide for her and Tierra.

I felt a tremendous sense of relief when the recruiting process was over. Not a day had passed in months when someone—a stranger, friend, teacher, family member, anyone—didn't ask where I would be going to college. You will be the first to know, I'd promise.

I could now focus on other concerns, such as trying to make it through my last year of high school. Up to that point, I had avoided any potential pitfalls that might prevent me from graduating and getting out of that place. That didn't stop me from worrying.

Until the last minute, literally.

On the morning of graduation, I went with a teammate to a practice ceremony at the Sumter County Exhibition Center. Miss practice, they told us, and you won't walk with your class. I even stayed the night before at a house by the arena, where my teammate's sister lived. We didn't want to take any chances.

So, wouldn't you know it, we got into a car accident on the way to the auditorium. A woman born in 1918—that has stuck in my mind for some reason—was the one at fault, but we still had to remain at the scene to fill out a police report and never made it to the practice.

As my friend and I waited for the officers to let us go, my fears got the worst of me: *Will this accident keep me from going to the University of Connecticut? From making a life for myself?*

Get a grip, I told myself. *A minor car accident won't keep you from graduating.* It just shows you the strange places your mind can go when you want something as badly as I did. Needless to say, I got my diploma.

Summer came and went. My five years in South Carolina, which sometimes felt like 50, were coming to an end, and I was ready to go.

And yet, I wouldn't be the person I am today if I hadn't gone through the struggles I had in those five years. It wasn't just about deciding to be a success instead of the failure others said I would be. It had to do with something more important.

When I first got to Ebenezer, I took it personally when other black kids criticized me for talking like a white kid. But over time I realized the problem wasn't me but them. If I'd let myself believe them, I might have become as hateful as some of them were, and possibly stayed that way for the rest of my life.

Now, whenever I run into the type of hatred and ignorance I dealt with 30 years ago—and believe me, I run into it a lot—it bothers me but I don't take it personally.

I was playing golf several years ago at a course in Connecticut I had gone to many times, when a guy I didn't know very well said to me: "How do you like playing the white man's game?"

I wasn't shocked. Just as I'm not shocked when I walk down the street and hear people lock their car doors because a black man is passing by. This has happened to me more times than I can ever remember.

Just as I'm not shocked when people pay me what they think is a compliment: "You speak so well," or, "You have such a great vocabulary."

Instead of becoming angry, I try to make a point.

"If I were a white person, would you say that to me?" I ask them.

There's usually no response. Seeing the look on their face, however, I know I have given them something to think about.

But back then, I wasn't so aware of all this. I was only starting to immerse myself in the types of challenges that would befall a young black basketball player.

There would be many more to come.

5

WHAT WAS IN STORRS FOR ME

I showed up on campus early, a week or so before the others.

That's always been my habit. Be the first to check out the new scene, and you'll have it down while everyone else is still struggling to find their way.

Take practice at UConn, which started at 3:30. I was there early enough to get my ankles taped, stretch, and get a few shots up. And being there long before you *have* to be there, I would realize later on, shows how serious you are, which, in turn, makes the coaches notice.

Same goes for arriving at Storrs. In those initial days, I got lost on more than a few occasions, but that was how I got my bearings, and it wasn't long before I felt as if I had been on campus forever. I knew where to eat and shop and where my classes were. I was determined not to be the typical freshman who stumbles around the first day of class, checking his map over and over.

That's not to suggest I didn't have concerns about the new life I was embarking on. On the plane to Hartford, having left behind the women most dear to me—Rosalind, Tierra, Mom, and my sisters, Kim, Talisha, and Kristie—I'd sensed, for probably the first time, how lonely I might be. Perhaps going to school so far away wasn't the smartest decision after all.

Fortunately, when I was greeted at the airport by assistant coach Leitao—carrying only $200 in my pocket and a trash bag filled with my entire wardrobe because I could not afford a suitcase—any concerns went away. It reminds me of the times I stepped to the free-throw line, scared to death I was going to miss. Once the ball was in my hands and I went through my routine, the fear was gone. *I got this*, I told myself.

One day on campus during those first weeks stands out. There was nothing unusual about the day, really, and come to think of it, that was the point. I woke up around 5:30, lifted weights, took a quick shower, and ate breakfast. Then I did something I had not done before, and I don't recall what inspired me. I put on a tie and sweater, raced out the door, and arrived in plenty of time for my 9:00 AM speech class.

"Why are you dressed up?" the girl next to me asked.

"Because I'm ready," I said.

It took going to class, with roughly a dozen other men and women my age, each on a journey of their own, for it to sink in: *This is no dream, Ray. You are a college student. You are in control of your destiny.*

I worked hard to get to that moment, and yet a part of me had believed it would never happen. Either I'd make some huge mistake, like a few guys I knew in high school, or something outside my control would lead to my downfall. A kid our family knew, in fact, who was the top running back in Sumter, was killed in a car accident several months after he was offered a scholarship to Clemson.

No longer was it about being the first Allen to make it to college; my sister Kim had enrolled at Benedict College in Columbia the year before. Though I did think a lot about all the black people in the history of this country who didn't get an opportunity like this, and the responsibility I now felt to make the most of it. Which meant, aside from keeping up with my studies, giving everything I could to the game of basketball, the reason I was able to be there in the first place.

The coaches were not kidding when they'd said I'd have to work hard from day one. I'd never trained for basketball before; I didn't think you had to. You just went out and played. Those days were over.

They liked to run us, and I mean a lot, which made the cross-county meets I ran in high school seem like Sunday strolls. Most grueling was the route known as Cemetery Hill—it went through a cemetery—that we were forced to run every Saturday. No one ever wanted to go on that thing. No one sane, that is. It started with a sharp incline, until it leveled off after about a mile. The farther you went, the steeper the incline got. The coaches were messing with our minds, not just our bodies.

The first time I saw Cemetery Hill I didn't think it was a big deal. This was during my visit the year before, and I was in a car with Coach Calhoun, watching his players run.

How awesome that they are doing this together, I'd thought. *Now, that's a real team!* What I did not know was that it was mandatory.

As for Coach Calhoun, think of him as a general on the battlefield. You could almost hear him saying: "Gentlemen, we have an enemy combatant out there, and we got to take him out before he takes us out. Dying is not an option."

He knew how to get our attention. In the minutes before practice began, we kept our eyes on the clock on the wall. Because when it struck 3:30, and not a minute later, the door would swing wide open and Coach would come through, pad and pen in his hand.

"Guys, we have a lot of work to do," he'd say. Every single day.

And when he said it, we had better be clapping, ready to give our all, and more. Or else.

"You guys don't want to be here?" he'd ask if just one person did not appear enthusiastic enough. "Get on the line."

Get on the line. The four words we dreaded most.

Those four words meant another form of running, as punishing as Cemetery Hill. We referred to it as "28s" because of what we would have to do in 28 seconds or less. There was another term for it—"suicides." In 28 seconds, we had to run from the baseline to the free-throw line and back to the baseline. Then from the baseline to half-court, and back to the baseline.

Follow me so far?

Then to the far free-throw line and back to the baseline. Then to the far baseline, until you finally finish at the baseline where you started.

In 28 seconds!

Most of the guys were able to do it, but that wasn't enough to satisfy Coach Calhoun, oh no. Everyone had to do it, or everyone would have to do it again. That was a problem for us, due to Eric Hayward, our six-foot-seven forward. Eric was, to put it delicately, a bit on the deliberate side. Okay, slow. No way could he finish in 28 seconds. So, to get out of the gym before the semester ended, we used to carry him across the line.

We still didn't always make it in 28 seconds, but that was not the point. We were becoming a team, no longer 14 individuals with 14 agendas, and the angrier we were at him for making us run, the more we bonded with one another. Before long, we realized that we could achieve more than we ever thought was possible. Coach Calhoun was similar to Coach Smith, making sure we didn't give up when giving up would have been easy. And if there were times I felt he went too far, I didn't say a word. I was already in a battle, with myself, every day on that court. Give up just once, and I might give up again, and again.

A few did give up, as you would expect, eventually transferring to other schools. I could've predicted who they would be by how they complained instead of doing what they were told to do. They assumed that because they were talented, they merely had to show up.

Not under Coach Calhoun.

To be on his good side, no simple feat, you had to work hard in practice, make it to class on time, be at study hall, and, guess what, do it all over again the next day.

That reminds me of my first practice. After it ended, Coach Leitao saw something he didn't like.

"Coach," Leitao told Coach Calhoun, "the freshman didn't sweat. He obviously didn't work hard enough."

Was he messing with me? I had worked extremely hard. The reason I didn't sweat was because the gym was air-conditioned and I was used to the humidity from being in the South. I worked so hard I was dying to get a drink of water, only to be stopped by Kevin Ollie, a teammate.

"Stay away from that water bottle," Kevin warned. "You can't just drink water whenever you feel like it. He's got to tell you that you can get it."

In any case, I have no idea whether Coach Calhoun ever responded to Coach Leitao about my not sweating enough. I hurried off the court and did not turn back.

Off the court, the closeness I saw between the players during my visit the year before was genuine, and being part of a group for the first time since I was a boy in California meant the world to me. I would do anything for my new friends.

Take the party underneath the Student Union freshman year, which a lot of football players attended. Not good. The football players at UConn always seemed to be envious of the basketball players. There were 14 of us, roughly 50 of them, and we received most of the attention. There was a dispute over—what else?—some girl and being the mature grown-ups we were, we decided to settle it with our fists. I was ready. It wasn't as if I'd never been in a fight before.

Except my teammates didn't want my help.

"Get out of here," they said. "Go back to the dorm."

"No, no, let's do it," I pleaded.

Their reasoning was this: It was one thing if we got in trouble; we were known for not always behaving well. Yet, if Coach found out that Ray, who had a stellar reputation, was involved, he was really going to make us pay. I certainly did not seek any special favors, but then I thought: *These guys hold me in high regard and I should respect that.*

On the other hand, there was one thing I wouldn't do with them.

That was drinking. Were there times I wished I could've joined them? You bet. Until I saw them hungover the morning after. To their credit, not once did they make me feel bad for staying away. They knew I was doing what was right for me. If I didn't succeed in basketball, I wanted it to be because I was not good enough, not because I drank too much.

I thought I was good enough, although I couldn't be certain. Not until the second game of the season, against Virginia in Charlottesville. Virginia, if you remember, was the school that sent a letter indicating they were no longer interested in recruiting me. I was eager to show them what they were missing. Members of my family also made the trip from South Carolina, and I didn't want to disappoint them.

How motivated I was, though, wouldn't influence Coach Calhoun one bit in deciding on the amount of playing time I'd have. He had a game to win, a big game. The Cavaliers were ranked number 12 in the nation. We were unranked. Beating them, on their court no less, would make a statement.

Loud and clear: UConn 77, Virginia 36.

No one saw it coming, although I couldn't be sure if they were that bad or we were that good. We pressed them on every possession, and they couldn't adjust. I scored 20 points off the bench, while the other reserves also played well, which was a welcome sign. In the first game of the year, against Towson, we won by 40, but that was because our starters dominated. You can't count on that game after game. Sooner rather than later, the bench would have to come through. I saw no reason why the bench couldn't be as integral to our success as the starting five. I felt that strongly about every team I was on.

One of those starters was Doron Sheffer, a 21-year-old freshman from Israel. I'll never forget the first time I saw Doron. I was shooting baskets in the gym when he walked in. He was six-foot-five, the same height I was, and also a guard. My immediate thought: *They have me. What do they need this guy for?* I wasn't threatened so much as driven to prove myself. Coach would start the one who was playing the best, and I was confident that would be me.

And though it turned out not to be me, I didn't mind one bit. Doron made us better, and that's what mattered. He averaged about 12 points and five assists a game and was the Big East Freshman of the Year. Besides, I was contributing as well, averaging 12.6 points, and when we were on the court at the same time, we clicked. Doron would drive past his defender and throw the ball to me in the perfect spot, and that makes a big difference in getting up a good shot.

I never forgot to work hard, though a reminder here and there didn't hurt. Like the time I was in the gym the first month and saw Donyell Marshall, our best player, and Scott Burrell, who had left school the year before and had been drafted by the Charlotte Hornets, shoot jumper after jumper. I couldn't take my eyes off them. They didn't miss.

How could I be that consistent? I knew the answer, of course. Practice. Practice. Practice.

Another time, I was taking a few shots, some as I stood still, others as I jumped, while Karl Hobbs, one of our assistant coaches, watched closely.

Until he had seen enough.

"Young fella," he said, "you just can't shoot a stand-still shot and not jump because now you're going to go against seven-footers who will be able to block your shot. You have to shoot the same way every time."

What Coach Hobbs said helped enormously. From then on, I made sure that I jumped whenever I took a shot. My shots were rarely blocked.

The win in Charlottesville put us at number 21 in the nation. Did we deserve it? It was too soon to tell.

I did, however, find out something else important that night. I found out what people in South Carolina thought of me, and it was what I suspected.

"I didn't know you were good," Rosalind said when I saw her briefly afterward. She quickly corrected herself. "I mean, I knew that you were good, but I thought you were good for Sumter, South Carolina, just better than the guys around there. I didn't know you would be this good at this level."

People told her I'd be back in four years and that no one from Dalzell ever amounted to anything. She believed them. I wasn't angry with her, not in the least. Besides, by this point Rosalind and I were beginning to grow apart, even if a formal breakup was a ways off. It wasn't that we didn't love each other, but it's extremely difficult to maintain a long-distance relationship, at that age especially. I could not go 50 yards on campus without running into a girl I wished

I could've gotten to know better. If only I wasn't involved with someone else.

As for the team, another key test came on the road, against Seton Hall. I was looking forward to it, but not just the game itself. I was excited about the trip *to* the game.

Soon after our bus crossed Connecticut into the state of New York, there it was, the Big Apple, as magical as I imagined it. I gazed out the window and couldn't believe it. There were actual living, breathing New Yorkers on the streets, and I wanted to get out and walk with them and talk to them for a little while, to be one of them.

But before I knew it, we were driving over the George Washington Bridge, heading to New Jersey, where Seton Hall is located. I kept looking behind me at the skyline until we arrived at the hotel in Secaucus. Seeing the city would have to wait.

I was scared to death leading up to the game. This was the Big East, the big-time, the stage I asked for, and now it was . . . here!

Yet once I stepped onto the court, the anxieties disappeared. The court was the same as any, and my responsibilities the same: get open, make shots, and stop the man I was guarding. Mission accomplished. The final: Connecticut 82, Seton Hall 66. I scored 17 points, 13 in the second half.

By late December, we were 7-0, ranked number 14. I couldn't figure out for the life of me why this team had struggled so much the season before. The only theory that made sense was that our year's leaders, Kevin Ollie, Donyell Marshall, and Donny Marshall (no relation), were more determined than the year before's.

"We're not losing anymore," they vowed. "We know our

way around, and we're going to make something out of these last two years of college."

In any case, off to Hawaii we went for a holiday tournament to extend our winning streak. To move up higher in the rankings. To enjoy a little sunshine. To . . .

Fall flat on our face.

After knocking off the University of Texas–Arlington, we lost to that powerhouse from the Mid-American Conference, Ohio University, 85–76. Having Donny kicked out with seven minutes left in the first half didn't help our cause, but that was no excuse. We stunk up the joint, simple as that—missing open shots, committing turnovers, getting out-hustled for every loose ball.

Not to let us off the hook, but Ohio was a much better team than people realized. They had a good point guard and a six-foot-eight, 250-pound power forward, Gary Trent, known as "the Shaq of the MAC." The nickname was appropriate; he was an absolute beast. We tried everything we could, including hacking the guy. Nothing worked. The loss, as it turned out, was what we needed. We'd become a little cocky. I don't recall us even having a scouting report on them.

The next day in Hawaii, we started another streak, with a win over Tennessee Tech. This streak would reach 10, carrying us to number 5, before a loss at Syracuse in early February. Seven of the 10 came in the Big East, including a win over St. John's in the Gahhhhh-den. At last, I was able to spend time in the city that never sleeps.

The rest of the guys also couldn't wait to do some exploring—not, however, until we heard from our camp counselor, Coach Calhoun, who summoned us to his hotel room.

"This is the best city in the world," Coach told us. "It's going to be one of the greatest experiences of your life."

With $60 in our pockets, the cash each of us were given for the road trip, Donny, our center Travis Knight, a few others, and I found our way to Times Square. Seeing the hordes of people and the bright lights, I can say without exaggeration, was one of the first times I felt truly alive.

There, we came upon the type of character you could find only in New York. He was operating a shell game, you know, where you hide a small ball under a cap. One look at the group of us—deer-in-the-headlights teenagers from the boonies—and the dollar signs in his head lit up.

Especially when he saw Travis, a white dude.

"Does anyone know where the ball is?" the guy asked.

Travis bit.

"I know where it is," he said.

Travis pointed, and the ball was right where he said it was. He thought he was so smart. The guy, of course, had the big fella on the hook now. He moved the caps around and asked again:

"Do you know where the ball is?"

Travis didn't hesitate. "I know."

Except this time, before he would lift the caps, he asked Travis to show him he had $60 and place it where he thought the ball was.

"No, no, no, I'm out of this," he insisted.

We insisted otherwise—well, Donny did. He somehow got Travis to open his wallet, and when he did, Donny took the $60 and placed it on the table. I don't have to tell you that was the last Travis ever saw of that $60. The ball, obviously, was under a different cap. Travis looked as if he was going to cry. Welcome to New York City, boys.

Hey, at least Travis, and the rest of us, avoided any real trouble that day and left the city in an excellent mood, with the St. John's victory. We kept rolling from there, and although we were knocked off by Providence in the Big East semis, we finished 27-4 and were awarded the No. 2 seed in the NCAA Tournament East Regional. A national championship was not out of the question.

There is, however, absolutely no margin for error in March Madness. Mess up in any way at the wrong time—a turnover, an ill-advised shot, a failure to box out your man, etc.—and you're likely to be going home, and I don't care how much talent you have.

That's what happened to us in the regional semifinal against Florida. It was a battle the entire way, but with just 3.4 seconds to go, we were in position to win the game and move on. Donyell, our can't-miss NBA prospect, was about to shoot two free throws, the score tied at 57. A few months earlier, he set a conference record with the most free throws in a game, hitting 20 of 20. Once he knocked down these two, or just one, we'd only have to make sure that nobody pulled a Christian Laettner on us and we'd secure a spot in the Elite Eight.

Donyell missed the first, and the Gators called a time-out. No problem. Icing a big-time player like Donyell wouldn't do any good.

He missed, naturally, and we lost, 69–60, in overtime. Losing was difficult enough, but then we had to deal with a report in the school newspaper that Donyell had been out partying the night before in Coconut Grove, an upscale Miami neighborhood. Even if it was true, and I'm not suggesting it was, it would not have been why he missed the free throws. Our game didn't begin until 10, the following night. Donyell just missed them, plain and simple.

Either way, I didn't let the loss keep me down for long. Given how dedicated our coaches were, I was convinced we'd return in the fall stronger than ever.

Although I came off the bench the entire season, I still received plenty of playing time and ended up as the second-leading scorer, behind Donyell. The effort I gave in practice had paid off, and for that, Coach Calhoun deserves a ton of credit. It wasn't just what he put us through day after day; it was what he said to me on one particular day that got through like nothing else.

I was walking off the court with a couple of teammates when he pulled me aside. It had been another long, exhausting workout, and I was looking forward to a little downtime.

"Did you make 100 percent of your shots today?" Coach asked.

"What do you mean?"

"Did you make 100 percent of your shots?"

What was I to tell him? Sure, Coach, I was perfect, just like I'm perfect every day. I'm actually insulted you didn't notice.

All kidding aside, his point was impossible to miss: if I was so intent on being a special player, in college and, hopefully, at the next level, I would have to make sacrifices others weren't willing to make.

"No," I told him. "I didn't make 100 percent of my shots."

He grinned and didn't say another word. I told the guys

I'd see them later, went back on the court, and, with a ball boy helping out, took shots for another half-hour. From that day forward, I took shots every day after practice officially ended.

Would I have preferred to go off with my teammates? No question. But I didn't want to look back someday and ask: What if I had put the extra hours in?

For example, there was my roommate during freshman year, Kirk King, a six-foot-eight forward from Louisiana. Kirk, also a freshman, had a body like a tight end. There was greater anticipation about him coming to Connecticut than there was about me. But while I stayed in the dorm every night, resting or hanging with friends, he often felt the need to be somewhere else, and because of his split focus, there have probably been times when Kirk, who didn't make it to the NBA, asks himself: *What if?* I know that would have haunted me forever.

Of course, there were occasions that first year when I wasn't pleased with how I handled the ball. So I decided to take the ball with me everywhere. Seriously, it didn't leave my side. In junior high, you may remember, I dribbled the ball day after day in the yard and across the street. That was nothing compared to what I did this time.

I took the ball to class. To the cafeteria. To bed, I kid you not. I came up with the idea from a movie I saw where a running back prone to fumbling carries the football with him wherever he goes so he'll become more comfortable with it during games.

It worked. My ball handling improved, which led to me getting off better shots. In the next game, against Hartford, I scored 28 points, a career high, going 11 of 20 from the field. Although it might've looked strange to teachers and students alike, what did I care? I was on a mission.

The summer after freshman year, I took part in the US Olympic Festival in St. Louis. I scored 28 in the opener, making four of seven three-pointers, and got 12 rebounds. I was only getting started. We won the silver medal, and I was the festival's leading scorer, breaking a record set by none other than Shaquille O'Neal. It gave me a huge boost. I was confident that if I had to, I could carry a team.

I wouldn't have to. Not yet, anyway. While we lost Donyell, who skipped his senior season to turn pro, we were loaded, with Kevin and Donny now seniors. I was expected, however, to take on more of the scoring burden, a challenge I looked forward to.

Speaking of challenges, we got a big one in our second game, against the Duke Blue Devils. We were the underdog. They were Duke. We were Connecticut. Nothing more needs to be said.

Except this: UConn 90, Duke 86. I led us with 26 points, Kevin adding 24. We were a step ahead of them the whole way.

If only that week had gone more smoothly for me away from the court.

Since the game, at the Palace of Auburn Hills in Michigan, was set for a Tuesday, we left Storrs on Monday, which meant I would have to miss a biology exam. No problem. I'd make it up when I got back.

Big problem.

The teacher told me I couldn't make it up no matter what my excuse was, and by flunking the exam, which was a large percentage of the grade, I flunked the class. Worse yet, I was put on academic probation. Never could I have imagined this would happen to me. I put a lot of time into my studies. I wasn't worried they'd take away my scholarship, although I understood I was being watched closely, and if I didn't keep my grades up, I could be in trouble. To be safe, I made arrangements to take several classes in the summer.

Meanwhile, the win against Duke was not an aberration. Over the next couple of months, we didn't lose once, rising to number 2 in the country. We were proud of ourselves but didn't get too carried away. I never heard any of us talk about being the first team since Bobby Knight's Indiana squad in 1975–1976 to go undefeated. We knew we could lose to anyone, at any time.

It happened in January, when Kansas crushed us, 88–59, in Kansas City. They grabbed a 20-point lead at halftime and didn't look back. We shot a horrible 26 percent from the field, and our press, for a change, didn't disrupt the other team's rhythm one bit.

So we lost. Every team loses. Not every team, however, has Jim Calhoun as its coach, and Jim Calhoun hated losing as much as anyone I've been around.

Coach took it as a personal insult. To that man, everything was about competing, and not just in the games. In practice, he set up one-on-one free-throw shooting contests, the first player to 20 being the winner. I can't overstate how much I wanted to beat my opponent. Because if I didn't, Coach would banish me to the opposite end of the court with the other losers. It was not a good feeling. The winners would remain with him.

If that weren't humiliating enough, then came the inevitable ribbing. Coach was a master at that.

"I see you couldn't beat KO [Kevin Ollie] today, huh?" he would say. "That's not like you to be down there with the others. You're not supposed to lose."

His objective was to teach us to take losing as personally as he did. And guess what? He succeeded.

For my teammates, the first practice after the Kansas defeat was a killer. I got off rather easy: I had twisted my ankle, so instead of practicing, I received treatment in the training room. Hearing Coach yelling at everyone in the gym, I had never been so grateful to be away from the action.

The tough love worked. We won eight of our last 10 to finish 23-3 and found ourselves, if briefly, ranked number 1. Although Villanova beat us handily in the Big East tournament final, we felt good about our chances heading into the tournament that mattered most, the Big Dance.

Except, once again, we came up short, losing to UCLA, 102–96, in the Elite Eight. The loss wasn't as painful as the one to Florida the season before and the fact that the Bruins went on to win the national championship made it hurt even less. I also had nothing to be ashamed of. I scored 36 points, 18 in each half, in what was, to that point, the biggest game of my life.

In the weeks that followed, I began to hear whispers that I should forgo my last two years of college and make myself eligible for the NBA Draft. One story floating out there was that I would be a definite lottery pick if I declared. Whether that was true or not, the idea of going pro did not enter my mind for a second, no matter the amount of money I stood to earn. I was having too much fun to think about leaving the college environment just yet. I would have the rest of my life to be in the "real world."

I still had a lot to learn. If you go to the NBA, you better be good right away, or you might find yourself out of a job in a year or two. Then what? It boggles my mind whenever I hear of players who declare for the draft even if they're not projected to be higher than a second-round pick. Imagine what another year in college could do for their games—and for their lives. Because once they leave college, now they're really on their own.

One afternoon, I was in the gym with a teammate who seemed eager to work out with me. That was, until his girlfriend showed up as we were shooting jumpers.

"Babe, I need you to take me to work," she told him. "We have to leave now or I'm going to be late."

Without the slightest resistance, he put the ball on the floor.

"Dude, this is your job," I said. "You can't walk out like this."

And because I'm telling this story, you are right in assuming that he didn't listen to me. It should also come as no shock that he eventually transferred to another school.

After he left that day, I remained in the gym for another hour or so. You see, it is not enough just to arrive early. You also must stick around until your work is done.

6

SETTING THE STAGE

Two relationships that meant a lot to me both came to an end around the same time, in my sophomore year.

One was the relationship with Rosalind, my first love. She said she wanted to see other people. I knew how she felt.

In college, I met women almost every day who wanted to conquer the world. That wasn't Rosalind. She was content just where she was, and there's nothing wrong with that. Except I saw a different future for myself. It was unfortunate Tierra would never have both parents in the same house, but she'd have my unconditional love and support, as well as her mother's, and that's a lot more than many kids have.

The other relationship was between Mom and Dad. I

was in my dorm room when I heard the news they were filing for divorce, and my initial reaction was: it's about time. They had tried for years to recapture whatever it was the two of them once had, and they couldn't try forever. There was no point in taking any sides. Dad wasn't perfect; neither was Mom.

If you think these changes set me back for a second, you should know better by now. My junior year would be the toughest yet, but my attitude was equally tough: bring it on!

For once, I wanted to be the player other teams designed their defenses around. Only then, in how I responded to the attention, would I find out what I was truly made of. If I couldn't handle the pressure in college, it wouldn't say a lot for my prospects as a pro.

I wasn't exactly the man sophomore year. I averaged 21 points, but teams did not set out to stop me specifically; Donny and Doron, each averaging in double figures, also had to be accounted for. I was still sneaking up on people, even in the NCAA Tournament. That wouldn't be the case my junior year.

I knew I'd have to be even more dedicated to my craft. So I moved from the dorm to an off-campus apartment. I loved dorm life. It was exactly how it looked in the movies, hanging out in one another's rooms, just talking—about classes, friends, music, whatever came up. I lived on the fourth floor, which was all-male, while the floors above and below us were all-female. Now, however, as I became more known, hanging out wasn't as simple as it was freshman or sophomore year. Students asked me practically every day to sign one thing or another. That got old fast. I needed my own space.

Mind you, not entirely my own. I had a roommate, Travis Knight. You remember Travis. Last time we saw him he was out 60 bucks, another poor victim of the Big Apple. Travis was a great guy, but let's just say he wasn't the neatest person in the world, and I'm obsessed with neatness. If I'm on the golf course and see a gum wrapper on the fairway, I'll go out of my way to put it in the trash. I've never been officially diagnosed, but it wouldn't shock me to learn I have a mild case of OCD.

Travis drove me crazy. He always left his dirty dishes in the sink.

"Wash your dishes," I kept telling him, but he didn't listen. "Next time you do it," I promised, "I'm going to put the dishes on your bed."

One evening, he came home with a girl he was trying to impress and found a pile of dishes precisely where I told him they would be. Travis took it like a true sport, though, and never left a dirty dish in the sink again.

My nature was to try to get along with everyone. I didn't always succeed.

The summer before, I was a member of the US team at the World University Games in Japan. That was some team, with Tim Duncan, Othella Harrington, Chucky Atkins, and Austin Croshere, who would all go on to play in the NBA. Oh, and Allen Iverson, from Georgetown.

We were all pretty friendly with each other, until the night, strangely enough, we won the gold medal. Afterward, we were eager to celebrate, A.I. more than anyone.

"We leave in the morning," Iverson told the rest of us, "so no one had better go to sleep or else they're going to get pranked. No one."

So who passes out as soon as he gets back to the dorm? You guessed it.

I suggested that we put peanut butter and shampoo all over Iverson's hands and face. There was no shortage of volunteers.

Except Iverson ruined our plan by waking up before we were finished, and he wanted revenge. Which he got on everyone else, until it came time to go after me. Soon, he and I were wrestling on the floor, punches being exchanged. Believe it or not, he was seriously trying to hurt me.

Before I knew it, he grabbed a fire extinguisher and swung it at me. I ducked just in time. Muhammad Ali would have been proud.

"I'm going to get you back," Iverson vowed.

"Dude," I said, "it was just a game." Somehow I didn't think I got through to him.

He and I would have many battles over the years—on the court.

Some people may have gotten the idea that we hated each other; that's how intense those battles were. Nonsense. He wanted to beat me, and I wanted to beat him, and that's how it should be.

My junior year began the same way as the previous two years. With us as hot as any team in the nation.

After falling in our second game to number 10 Iowa, 101–95, in OT, we beat number 23 Indiana by 34 points and Northeastern by 47. By mid-February, we stood at 24-1, including 14-0 in the conference.

Then, at the Capital Centre in Landover, Maryland,

came the duel between number 3 UConn and number 11 Georgetown—and yours truly and Allen Iverson.

The Hoyas, to be sure, were far from a one-man team, as were we, and their coach was one of the best, John Thompson. Nearly seven feet tall, he intimidated the hell out of you, and his players took on his personality, especially on the defensive end, hounding you from one end of the court to the other. Like Coach Calhoun, he would have made a tremendous general. Coach Thompson got the better of us on that occasion: Georgetown 77, Connecticut 65. It was their press that won it for them, forcing us to commit 20 turnovers. On the offensive side, it was all Iverson: 26 points and six assists. I hit just five of 18, tying a season-low with 13 points.

Less than a month later, we faced Georgetown again, in the Big East tournament final at the Garden. The winner, in addition to bragging rights, would get a boost going into the Big Dance, set to begin a few days later. We played better in that game and trailed by only four points at the half. Even so, with four and a half minutes to go, the Hoyas were up by 11. We needed a spark, and fast.

And we got one, from Kirk King. Kirk made two baskets and two free throws to cut the deficit to five. Several possessions later, he scored on an emphatic dunk to slice it to one. When the Hoyas went to the free-throw line and missed the front end of a one-and-one, we had the ball with 44 seconds left.

Coach Calhoun called time. In the huddle, he didn't waver for a second. "I'm going to Ray," he said.

My first thought: *He believes in me.* He believed in me even though other guys, like Kirk, and Ricky Moore, our freshman guard, were having much better games. I was four of 19, having missed my last 14 in a row. Nobody would have blamed him if he were to go with someone who had a hot hand.

"Ray, you'll come off the screen, and then you'll have the whole side to operate," Coach said.

Once he showed confidence in me, no way was I going to let him, and the team, down.

With 18 seconds left, I got the ball from Ricky, turned to the right, and drove in the direction of the basket. Iverson bumped me, while Jerome Williams, the Georgetown forward, edged over to help. I thought for a split-second about getting it to Rudy Johnson, my teammate, who was open in the corner, but he pulled his hands back.

Now I was in trouble—in the air and off-balance. So, with no other option, I threw it up in the vicinity of the hoop, and the ball bounced off the rim, then the backboard, and in!

Connecticut 75, Georgetown 74.

It wasn't over yet. There were 14 seconds to go, an eternity for Allen Iverson. Everybody remembers his rant about practice but I can't think of a player who was more fearless. Only six feet tall, at most, he had a lot to prove, and, year after year, he did.

Iverson missed that time, thank goodness, a fadeaway behind the free-throw line. Williams grabbed the rebound and had a great chance from just a few feet away. But he missed, as well.

Then it was over. In those final four and a half minutes, we outscored the Hoyas, 12–0. We were the Big East champs. The title we craved most was next, and as the number 1 seed in the Southeast Regional in Indianapolis, we couldn't have felt more confident.

You wouldn't know it by how we played in the first two rounds. Yes, we got past Colgate and Eastern Michigan to reach the Sweet Sixteen for the third year in a row, but if we didn't pick up our game, we would come up short once again.

From Indianapolis, we went, ironically, to Lexington.

Once upon a time it looked like I might play in a lot of big games at Rupp Arena. Now, if we could win the next two, Rupp would forever be the place where I booked my ticket to the Final Four.

First, we had to get by the number 5 seed, the Mississippi State Bulldogs, which was no given. This was the team that had stunned Kentucky a few weeks before in the SEC tournament championship game. They had four players averaging double figures, including Erick Dampier, their six-foot-eleven center, who would spend 16 years in the NBA.

As it turned out, their guard, Darryl Wilson, was the one who killed us. He hit five three-pointers in a row, seven altogether, scoring 27 points in a 60 55 win. I killed us as well, making only nine of 25, the most crucial miss with 12 seconds to go, a three that would have tied the game. I also missed both of my free throws.

Like the loss to Florida two years earlier, this one hurt. It was a game we should have won, though I have often asked myself: Did we *want* to win? Nonsense, you say. Of course you wanted to win. Maybe, but a part of us wanted to go home, which is what we should have done between the games in Indianapolis and Lexington. Coach was looking to avoid any distractions, though, and that's why we stayed away.

I can see his point, but sometimes you need a pat on the back, and we would have gotten that on campus. What does this have to do with the way we played? Impossible to say, but I can tell you that, after the game, the guys were as happy to go to return to Storrs as they would have been to remain on the road for another couple of days, and you can't split your focus if you hope to win a championship.

In any case, what the future would hold was not on my mind as I got off the court at Rupp. Clearly, however, it was on the mind of Stephon Marbury, whose Georgia Tech team was about to take on Cincinnati in the next game.

"See you in the draft," Stephon told me.

Meanwhile, I went to class like everybody else. I was a student-athlete, not an athlete-student. At least, that was the plan. Every time I showed up, though, the other students gave me funny looks.

"Why are you here?" they asked.

Heck, even the professors were puzzled. A week or so later, it finally hit me: *Why am I here?* By this point, all anybody wanted to know was if I was going to turn pro or come back for my senior year. It reminded me of high school, when everyone kept asking where I was going to college.

To many, there was no doubt. *Ray, you are the Big East Player of the Year. You're one of the best guards in the country. You will be a top-five pick in the draft. You'll be set for life. How can you not go?*

Everything they said was true. But first, I wanted to see if I could make the case to stay.

One person who didn't hesitate to make it was Jim Calhoun.

"You don't want to go yet," Coach told me. "You'll be

with a lot of grown men, hanging out, doing God knows what. Plus, you could certainly use another year in college to get better."

I looked up to Coach Calhoun and appreciated what he was saying. Whenever I strayed, even a little, from doing what I needed to improve my game ("Did you make 100 percent of your shots today?"), he was there to set me straight. None of what happened later could have happened without him. Plus, I didn't doubt for a moment he was telling me the truth. You can always get better.

On the other hand, some members of my family were excited about the prospects of me turning pro, though Mom said she would be pleased with whatever I decided. God bless her.

The days flew by. At times, I felt I was close to announcing my decision. Others, I wasn't so sure. Then came the day that made it clearer to me than ever, and from a most unlikely source. I was walking on campus when I bumped into my former anthropology professor, Mr. Magubane. An expert on the draft he was not.

"Mr. Allen, what are you doing with your future?" he asked.

"I don't know," I told him.

"Mr. Allen, look around you," he went on. "This university has been here since the 1800s. And it will be here long after you're gone."

That's all he said, but it was enough. For the longest time, I worried people might think poorly of me if I chose making money over getting my degree, but he made me see that I could earn a degree anytime. Besides, there has always been a stigma attached to the black athlete who leaves college early. Name one white athlete who was criticized for taking the money.

In the end, there was no case I could make to stay. I could only make the case to go.

Leaving Connecticut was difficult. I had shown up at the airport in Hartford three years earlier with a trash bag full of clothes, $200 in my pocket, and no guarantees. Now, after the work I put in and the lessons I learned from Coach Calhoun and his staff, I was going out into the world with a chance to live my dream. But it was more than that. They taught me to be a man, not just a basketball player. For that, I will be forever grateful.

The bonds I created with my teammates were the strongest of my life, and still are. We came from different parts of the country, and although we'd reached a certain level of success before we got there, there was still a lot to learn. The learning didn't come easy, and for each of us, there were times we didn't think it would ever come. In those times, we were there for one another. Always.

Sure, I wished we had played in a Final Four. We certainly had our chances. If Donyell had made one of the free throws against Florida. If UCLA hadn't been on a roll. If I had hit the three against Mississippi State. Coach used to tell us you have to be lucky to get there. We weren't. Yet, even if I'd been in a Final Four with Kentucky or another school with a rich tradition, I wouldn't have the satisfaction I do today from playing for UConn. I helped build something special.

In the spring of 1999, I was in the stands at Tropicana Field in St. Petersburg, Florida, when the Huskies captured the first of their four national championships, beating Duke,

77–74. I felt a part of that triumph belonged to me and everyone who had played at the University of Connecticut.

The decision to go to UConn and, three years later, to leave UConn was mine and mine alone. However, by putting my name in the 1996 NBA Draft, I'd be back where I was as a kid, going where someone told me to go.

Barring a trade, it would be one of four cities: Philadelphia, Toronto, Vancouver, or Milwaukee, the teams with the first four selections. No one figured I would last any longer.

In the days leading up to the big day, June 26, I visited each place so that the teams could put me through a workout. It was one thing to see a player on film, another to see him in the flesh. The importance of making the right decision can't be overstated. The wrong one can set a franchise back years and cost a general manager his job.

Two visits stood out: Toronto, for what did not happen, and Milwaukee, for what did.

In Toronto, I met with the legendary Pistons guard Isiah Thomas, a part owner and executive with the Raptors.

"I want to see you run from here to there," Isiah said, pointing to a spot on the court about 30 yards away. Whatever you say, Mr. Thomas.

Once I got there, I awaited further instructions. They never came.

"I don't need you to do anything else," he said. "I know what you can do."

Well, that certainly didn't make me believe I'd end up in Toronto. If you're going to invest a lot of money into your so-called player of the future, you better see every part of his skill set. The NBA doesn't give you do-overs.

If you think the Toronto "workout" was out of the ordinary, wait till you hear what took place in Milwaukee.

Shortly after I got to the practice facility, Mike Dunleavy, the team's GM, asked me to play a game of one-on-one against Chris Robinson, a guard from Western Kentucky, who the Bucks were thinking about picking in the second round.

No problem. While playing one-on-one is hardly the fairest test of an individual's value in a team game, I figured Dunleavy might learn a thing or two about me he would not spot in other drills. Chris had a flight to catch, so I knew we wouldn't play for long. We went at each other pretty hard.

Once Chris took off, I figured Dunleavy would put me through a more conventional workout.

Guess again.

"Let's play, you and I," he said.

You and I? Was he out of his mind? Mike Dunleavy had been a decent player in his day, except his day was long gone; he was 42. What he could possibly gain from playing someone half his age, I didn't have a clue.

Whatever he was thinking, I couldn't say no, could I? And no, I don't remember the score, if there was one.

Afterward, I met with Senator Herb Kohl, who owned the team. The senator and I hit it off, but as I left town, I was still trying to figure out what Dunleavy had been up to.

In any case, that was it for my visits. Minnesota, picking fifth, asked me at the last minute to come in for a workout, but I declined. My family was already in New York for activities related to the draft, which was to take place in New Jersey.

Besides, the Timberwolves had a talented young shooting guard, J. R. Rider. They didn't need me.

One team that did was the Boston Celtics, at number 6. I was in my hotel room, just hours before the draft, when a call came from Red Auerbach, the president of the Celtics. Red *was* the Celtics, dating back to the early 1950s, before they started winning championships, eight in a row at one point. He said they would take me if I was still on the board. I was blown away.

Whatever my fate might be, I didn't have to wait long. I took a seat in the green room at the Continental Airlines Arena with the others whose lives were about to change forever.

Around 7:30 PM, before a national audience on TNT, Commissioner Stern walked to the podium and began to recite the names:

Allen Iverson to the Sixers at number 1. No surprise there. You want to get your fan base excited, you take the most exciting young player in the game.

Marcus Camby, a center from the University of Massachusetts, to Toronto at number 2. No surprise there either. The Raptors needed a big. I wondered what kind of workout Isiah put him through.

Shareef Abdur-Rahim, a small forward from Cal, to Vancouver at number 3. Good move. Shareef is a baller. The Grizzlies took the whole process extremely seriously. In my workout with them, they looked at my vertical leap and how many pounds I could bench-press, and they put me through a few agility tests. From what I heard, they were that thorough with everyone.

Now the proceedings were about to really get interesting. The Bucks, I assumed, would pick me, in spite of the unusual day I spent there. Yet the moment I heard the commissioner call out, "Stephon Marbury," all I could think was: *Oh my God! I can't believe it! I'm going to be a Celtic!* There was no way Minnesota, picking right before Boston, was going to take me, not after I wouldn't show up for the workout.

If that's the case, I asked myself, *then why are the cameramen from TNT rushing to my table?*

They knew something I didn't.

"With the fifth pick in the 1996 NBA Draft," Stern said, reading from a card, "the Minnesota Timberwolves select Ray Allen from the University of Connecticut."

What? Someone must have handed him the wrong card. It happens. Look at the 2017 Academy Awards.

It was the right card. I was going to Minnesota, and now I had to pretend I was excited about it. I got up, handed Tierra to my father, put on a Timberwolves cap, and, wearing a cream suit I bought for the occasion, went to the stage to shake hands with the commissioner, smiling the whole time.

Before I knew it, I was being interviewed by TNT's Craig Sager.

"Minnesota's a great city," I said, meaning Minneapolis, of course. "They have a great organization, and I'll be ready to play there next year."

Was I a good actor, or what?

My next interview was with a television reporter from Minnesota. Gee, how much longer would I have to keep up this charade?

While I was giving another cliché answer, some league official interrupted. "Sorry, but we have to pull him out of this," he said.

I had been traded for Marbury. Ultimately, the Bucks

would also receive center Andrew Lang. Stephon and I exchanged hats in front of the cameras, and the draft went on. Some draft that was too, with names such as Kobe Bryant, Steve Nash, Derek Fisher, and Antoine Walker.

You'd think I'd be relieved, wouldn't you, Milwaukee being a lot better than . . . Minnesota? I wasn't. Thirty minutes into my NBA career, and already somebody didn't want me. I felt even worse when I found out fans who showed up to watch the draft at the Bradley Center in Milwaukee, where the Bucks played, booed the deal. This was the Midwest, where people knew very little about the Big East. They knew plenty about Stephon, on the other hand, and the teams he played against in the ACC.

Once I returned to the hotel, I began to cry. My family couldn't figure out what was wrong.

"Don't you want to celebrate?" they asked.

Celebrate what? Being traded? Being booed? The biggest night of my life, and I couldn't remember when I felt as devastated.

I needed to get the hell out of there. I'd go for a drive, but not by myself. I'd pick up someone I met the day before.

Shannon and I met at the All Star Café in Manhattan, where I went for a party related to the draft. I'd never seen anyone so beautiful.

Our first conversation didn't last long, but when I found out she was going afterward to the same club I was going to—fate always plays a role in romance, doesn't it?—I asked her to save a dance for me. She said she would.

I liked everything about her, including the fact that she knew nothing about basketball.

"Tomorrow I'm getting drafted," I told Shannon.

"I didn't know we were at war," she said. I swear, she wasn't trying to be funny.

We had that dance she promised and talked until it got late and we both had to go: me to get ready for my big day and she for hers. Shannon was a singer for an R&B group, Shades, and her first single, released by Motown, was hitting the stores. How fitting. I said good night and told her I'd call the next day.

Now the next day was here. As soon as I walked off the stage in New Jersey, I found a phone.

"I have to see you right away," I told her. "I can't leave town without seeing you."

I picked up Shannon at her apartment, and we drove to the pier in Jersey City to talk—me to talk, that is, and I whined more than I talked. I said how awesome it would have been if the Celtics had chosen me instead of winding up in Milwaukee. She was sympathetic, to a point.

"You're going to live your dream?" she asked. *Yup.* "Make a lot of money?" *Yup.* "Take care of your family?" *Yup.*

She didn't want to hear another word.

"*Buck* up, buttercup," she said, no pun intended.

That's another thing I appreciated about Shannon. She didn't have a problem expressing herself.

Time was getting away from us. It must have been around 2:00 AM, perhaps 3:00, when I dropped her back at her apartment.

In a couple of hours, I would be getting on a plane to Milwaukee to start the future I'd been dreaming about since I was 14, when I saw Michael Jordan on television and knew I wanted to be just like him.

7

THE BUCK STARTS HERE

Think Storrs, Connecticut, is in the middle of nowhere?

Try Oshkosh, Wisconsin, about 90 miles from Milwaukee, where the Bucks held training camp.

I don't want to sound petty. I know how many people would have traded places with me in a second, no questions asked. All I'm suggesting is that being in the NBA was not everything it was cracked up to be.

. Hotel. Practice. Hotel. Practice. You get the picture.

It went on like that day after day in Oshkosh, and it was no more glamorous when camp ended and the season began. As for those parties and fancy cars and celebrities they tell you about, if that was the life of a professional basketball player, it was the life in other cities, not Milwaukee.

Often, I didn't feel like I was in the league at all. We didn't draw big crowds at home, and on the road there was no Milwaukee Bucks Nation that came out to cheer us on. The Green Bay Packers owned the city, and state, and used to play games in Milwaukee into the mid-1990s. I felt I was back in high school, football being the sport that people were passionate about. Whenever my teammates and I ran into folks on our way to practice, the conversations would usually go something like this:

"You guys are tall. You must play basketball."

"We sure do."

"So you play for Marquette?"

"No, we play for the Bucks."

"That's nice."

And off they went, unimpressed.

After every game at the Bradley Center, I ordered a pizza and headed home to watch *The X-Files*. Did I know how to have a good time, or what?

On the road, we were the butt of jokes: all anybody knew of Milwaukee was that it was where Laverne and Shirley lived. We would hear the theme song from that sitcom whenever we ran out onto the court. That got old fast.

I didn't have much fun when I was playing either. Come to think of it, it was not much different from my early days at UConn when I was trying to find a way to fit in.

Except in one very important respect: in the NBA, you are on your own, unlike in college, where, between classes and hanging out with your buddies, there's a lot to take your mind away from any struggles you might be going through.

Have a tough shooting night? Well, you can't afford to think about it right now; you have an exam to study for.

The NBA was infinitely more difficult. I didn't know the system. I didn't know the offense. I didn't know the rules. Defense? Forget it. Seriously, how in the world was I going to contain scoring machines such as Reggie Miller and Mitch Richmond and Dell Curry—Steph's father—and the guy who wore number 23 for the Chicago Bulls?

Seeing Michael Jordan in person blew me away. I had been looking forward to it from the time I checked out the Bucks' preseason schedule at training camp and noticed an upcoming game with the Bulls at the United Center in Chicago. *This is actually happening*, I told myself.

The night was surreal. I was doing my normal stretching when the Bulls jogged onto the court, Michael the last to appear. The first thing to strike me was that he was a lot darker than I remembered seeing on TV, like a shadow. Before I could take it all in, the horn sounded and I found myself on the court with him before the jump ball . . . and, my God, he's headed right toward me!

"Ray," he said, extending his hand, "welcome to the NBA."

"Thank you," I said.

Holy shit, MJ knows my name. Not until later did it hit me that he, like any other opposing player, must have glanced at the scouting report. So of course he'd know my name.

As for the game itself, if my memory is correct, I scored nine points in the first quarter before Chris Ford, our coach, sat me down for the rest of the night. I was upset; I would have played the entire 48 minutes if he had let me.

Chris made sure I always remembered where I stood in the pecking order, referring to me as "rook." He subscribed to the old-school mentality many coaches believe in: Put the kid in his place. Remind him that he doesn't know any better.

Every possession, he'd tell me to "shoot the ball" or "dribble" or "bounce it." All I could think was: *Dude, can you please let me do my job?* It was hard enough trying to focus on the opponent and learn our schemes without listening to a coach yelling God knows what every other second. I finally wised up, walking to the other side of the floor, simply to get away from his badgering.

That didn't stop him.

"Go get rook," he would tell one of my teammates, and then get on my case all over again.

Instead of raising his voice, I wished he would've taken the time to calmly teach me. That's how you bring out the best in your players. In the NBA, or at any level of the game.

There were occasions, to be fair, when Coach Ford did teach me something. Whether he intended to or not.

Such as the time my alarm failed to go off—I had set it for PM instead of AM—causing me to miss a shootaround. He didn't start me that night against the Washington Bullets, which bothered me to no end. In his mind, if you miss practice, you must pay the consequences. In my 18 years in the league, I am proud to say, I was never late to a shootaround, or a practice, again.

Another time, we'd just lost and Vin Baker, our best player, was so disgusted that he dressed in a hurry and bolted from the locker room without a word to the press. Not interested in dealing with any questions myself, I took off too, and didn't give the matter a second thought. Chris would make sure I did.

"Rook," he told me after he heard complaints from report-

THE BUCK STARTS HERE

ers a few days later, "you don't want to be locked in as having a bad reputation in this league. You're a nice, well-meaning kid, and the media is going to have your back, or they're not. So, whenever you lose, you have to be man enough to own up to your faults. You have to speak on behalf of your team, if you ever want to be a leader."

From that moment on, I never ran from the media again, no matter how gut-wrenching any defeats were, and believe me, there were plenty.

"I could have played better," I would admit, or, "I turned the ball over too many times," or, "We didn't match the other team's sense of urgency." It didn't matter what I said, as long as I said something. A leader, I came to understand, is not just the player who scores the most points. A leader is also the one who accepts the blame even when—*especially* when—he doesn't deserve it. I played with a lot of guys who saw themselves as leaders. That's the last thing they were. They were willing to take the credit whenever the team was doing well, but when the team struggled, they vanished.

As a rookie, assuming that kind of responsibility wasn't my concern. You can't lead if you're still trying to find your way. Shannon was a tremendous help in those early months, with a bluntness I would come to rely on. She visited me in Milwaukee quite a bit, and having her around was something I looked forward to more than you can imagine.

"What would you say if I asked you to marry me?" I said.

"We barely know each other," she responded.

As it would end up, marriage was a ways off, which was the best thing for both of us. We had careers to build first. The fact that Shannon wanted to be successful in her own right was something else I admired about her.

There were things to admire about our team too—Vin and small forward Glenn Robinson, the number 1 overall pick from the 1994 draft, come to mind—but we still could not fare better than 33-49, finishing 36 games behind the Bulls. Yikes. Coach Calhoun taught me to hate losing, but I really didn't know what it felt like to lose until I got to the NBA. I lost a lot in those early years, and I never got used to it. The fans didn't either.

They had every right to boo, no doubt, but I thought they went over the top on more than a few occasions. Though, later on, I realized that they had a point, that some players didn't give 100 percent night after night. Which was the norm, sadly, in the NBA, unlike college. In college, with far fewer games, each one is an event. Conversely, a game between two teams in the NBA with losing records on a cold evening in January is not an event.

Even so, that's no excuse for a letdown. You're a professional athlete, getting paid a ridiculous amount of money, and every night someone is coming to see you for the first, and quite possibly, only time. To give them anything less than your absolute best is unforgivable.

Off the court, I was slowly adjusting to my surroundings. I stayed in Vin's home for a few months. He was like a big brother to me. I knew nothing about the city when I first got there: I didn't know where to eat, where to shop, where to see a movie. Nothing. So not having to find somewhere to live was one less task to worry about. By the time I moved into a place of my own, I was ready, thanks to Vin.

I also bought a house in Connecticut for my mother. She'd done everything for me, and I don't mean just the usual things that moms do for their kids. To see her in a home she owned, not an apartment she rented, made me happier than anything. Otherwise, I didn't spend much the first year. I drove a rental car a friend at a local dealership let me use, and because it snowed constantly, I never had to wash it.

Milwaukee, for all my griping those first few months, turned out to be the right place for me, like South Carolina was. And Storrs, for that matter.

I grew as a player and as a person. I'm not suggesting it wouldn't have happened somewhere else, but, in Milwaukee, because of the weather and lack of nightlife, I wasn't enticed to buy a fancier car or spend time in the clubs. Which wouldn't have helped me better prepare for Reggie Miller or Michael Jordan.

Nor would it have helped me better cope with whatever the press may say about me. Which could be anything, as I found out before I had even appeared in my first game.

SLAM magazine covered the highly touted 1996 draft class—"Ready or not . . . here they come!"—and predicted that Stephon Marbury was the most likely to be Rookie of the Year, and Shareef Abdur-Rahim the most likely to average 20 points per game. Fair enough. I, on the other hand, was deemed the most likely to "fade into obscurity."

I knew what "obscurity" meant, but wanting to be sure, I looked it up anyway, and man, was I pissed off. What would ever possess them to write that? I never bothered to find out, but like Kenny and those others who doubted me, I didn't forget. I still spoke to their writers as the years went on, but I always reminded them how angry I was about that article. As usual, being put down like that made me more motivated. I wasn't sure that was possible.

In year two with the Bucks, we struggled once again. There was at least a sense that the future would be better than the past. It couldn't be much worse.

In September, we had sent Vin Baker to Seattle in a three-team deal that included the Cavaliers, and while I looked up to Vin, it meant a bigger role for me in the offense, similar to when Donyell Marshall left for the NBA after my freshman year at UConn. I went from averaging 13.4 points per game to 19.5, second behind Glenn Robinson's 23.4.

That season I had another memorable chat with Coach Ford.

"You don't have a routine," he explained. "You just go out and do whatever and believe that will be enough. You need to find a routine and stick to it every night. You can't just run around."

He was right. I didn't have a routine because I didn't think I needed one. In college, the coaches created a routine for you, day after day. There was a set time for meetings, for watching film, for being on the floor, for stretching with the trainer, for joining the layup line, for study hall, and for eating meals. I think that covers everything.

That isn't the situation once you turn pro. Except for practices, shootarounds, traveling, and the games themselves, what you do with your time is up to you. Sounds pretty good, doesn't it?

It is, if you spend your time wisely, which I did. And, for a while in Milwaukee, I had company.

Each morning, two teammates, Michael Curry and Elliot Perry, both guards, and I met for breakfast at the hotel, taking turns on who picked up the check. Then we took a taxi to the arena, arriving roughly three hours prior to tip-off to get our shots up before the bigs showed up. Nothing personal against the bigs, but being in the paint, they get in your way and slow down your rhythm. Midrange, long range, free throws, we worked our way around the perimeter, with a rebounder tossing the ball to keep us in sync.

I was happy to have Michael and Elliot with me, as I would be later in my career when other players came to my workouts. Provided that they were in it for the long haul.

Some teammates, every so often, would ask: "Ray, can I shoot with you?"

"Sure," I told them, "but you can't just be here today. You have to be here every day." That was because, once you join me, you become part of my routine, and it would throw me off if you are in the gym one day and gone the next.

Michael and Elliot both left the Bucks in 1999, but I stuck to my routine, through my last game in 2014.

At times, my teammates could not figure out why I put in the extra effort, but there was no mystery. You get such a small window to make it as a professional athlete, you owe it to yourself to give it everything you have until age, the one opponent you cannot overcome, takes you down. I thought of my father, who may have been able to advance further in his career, and how I promised myself I would work as hard as I could.

Lots of players won't make the commitment simply because they don't want to be held to the same high standard for the rest of their careers. I get it. There were countless mornings I woke up in freezing, snowy Milwaukee, my back still aching from the game the night before, and asked myself: *Why not, just this one time, give yourself a break and stay in bed for another hour? What's the harm? No one will ever know.*

Only I would know, and if I skipped one time, I might skip another, and another, and would soon feel the difference come the fourth quarter, when my team needed me the most and the usual lift in my legs wouldn't be there. It's one thing to miss a free throw or a jump shot because, well, you miss; that happens. It's another to miss because you don't put in the work. That should never happen.

Each time I worked out for 30 minutes I felt like a new person, so when the game began, and other guys worried about making their shots and having enough stamina down the stretch, I was as relaxed as I could be. As strange as it may sound, I'd already played the game.

That doesn't mean I would automatically come through—the player guarding you is also a professional, with pride and talent—but whenever I didn't, it was not for lack of preparation.

A writer once asked me: "You had a bad game. How are you going to respond?"

"I didn't have a bad game," I said. "The ball just didn't go in the basket."

A bad game isn't necessarily when you shoot three for 15 or throw a few errant passes. That's because you can still contribute in numerous other ways to help the team.

To me, a bad game is when you come in unprepared, with little energy—*and* shoot poorly and commit turnovers.

At the same time, a good game isn't necessarily when you

shoot 11 of 15. The "experts" on TV will rave about a player who scores a lot of points, but is he helping out on defense? Is he taking the proper shot at the proper time in the flow of the offense? Is he bringing out the best in his teammates?

I don't mean to put down how important shooting is. I thought about shooting more than you can imagine. I *dreamed* about it. And, by the way, in those dreams, I always shot zero for something like 1,000, which meant I would have to leave for the gym earlier than usual in the morning—or the lab, as I called it. The idea was to get any negative thoughts out of my head as fast as possible. Once I got the work in and saw the ball fall through the net I could relax, knowing that I would be fine. For the next game at least.

Being prepared isn't just about getting your shots up and running on the treadmill; it's also about keeping track of your sleep and diet.

You can lie to yourself, but you cannot lie to your body. Your body remembers what you ate and how much sleep you got. Sure, you may get away with it for a game or two, or a whole season, if you're lucky, but it will catch up to you. It catches up to everyone. That goes for those who had outstanding, even borderline Hall of Fame careers.

I could always tell whenever the guys I played against weren't as prepared as they should have been. I'd be kicking it into another gear, or *rare air,* as I referred to it, while they'd be running out of gas chasing me from one side of the court to the other. And by sticking to a routine, I got to the point after a few years in the league where I knew any shot I took in the fourth quarter had a good chance of going in.

It's convenient to come up with excuses, and not just in basketball, and ignore the fact that the potential for your greatness is always in your control. I can't tell you how many players said they would join me for a workout, only to complain that their alarm did not go off or the traffic was bad. I don't want to hear it. You should know the traffic is bad at that time of day. Next time, leave a little earlier. Because, in the end, you show up or you don't.

And any time someone said: "God blessed you with this gift but he hasn't blessed me," it felt like a slap in the face. The gift, I told them, is the work I put in, day after day. I didn't grow up with a basketball in my hand given to me by God. God doesn't care if I can shoot a basketball. That's not what he has in store for me. He wants me to work as hard as I can to make myself, and everyone around me, better. He wants that for all of us.

People talk about who is blessed, and who isn't, to take themselves off the hook. *Why should I work harder? It won't do me any good.* I even heard players in the NBA say that. I was never surprised when they were out of the game within a year or two.

On the other hand, I saw guys who worked extremely hard, and that's why they stuck around the league for years. A prime example is Ben Wallace, the undersized center who played for the Pistons in the early to mid-2000s. Ben was not a real scoring threat, but by giving a total effort, night after night, he became one of the premier defensive players in the game. He accepted his role: clear the boards and get the ball to the playmakers. No wonder he earned the respect of his peers—and a ring, in 2004.

At times, I would show up to the gym too early, before the locker room was open. I'd have to find a security guard who would track down the ball kid, who had the key to the joint. Whatever it took.

Once, in Chicago, because the bus had yet to arrive with our workout clothes, it appeared I would have to wait a while. A locker room attendant then came up with a suggestion.

"Michael Jordan's in there," he said. "Maybe you could use some of his stuff. He's got a ton."

"Really?"

"Yeah, but you got to ask him."

I somehow got up the nerve, although I expected him to say no. I would not have blamed him. I was, last time I checked, a member of the opposing team.

How wrong I was. Michael couldn't have been more gracious, showing me a closet filled with nothing but shoes. The attendant was not exaggerating. There must have been 200, maybe 300, pairs in there. Funny, but I'd been in the league more than a year by then, and I was still amazed he knew who I was.

Sometimes, if I was aware that our opponent was planning to have a shootaround, I showed up even earlier, although that didn't always go over very well. It didn't matter that I had every right to be there. They treated me like I was a kid off the streets, not a player in the NBA.

"Hey, you can't be on the floor," somebody who worked for another team told me once. "We're going to have practice."

"I'll be here for 20 minutes and then I'll be gone," I pleaded.

He wouldn't budge.

Another time, when I was on the Heat and we were in Milwaukee for a playoff game, a Bucks representative kicked me and several teammates off the floor, though no one else was around. I argued, to no avail, and then it occurred to me: Why weren't any of their players on the court to prepare for such an important game?

Nothing put me more at ease than having the floor to myself. It gave me time to think. Not about the team we'd be facing that night, or the player I would be guarding—that would come later—but about my routine:

Was I getting enough lift in my legs? Should I shoot more? Run more? Was I missing anything?

By the time my teammates would show up for the shoot-around I was ready, and by no longer focusing on myself, I could focus on them. Any team, and it doesn't matter which sport, succeeds to the degree that each member helps the others.

As the 1997–98 season unfolded, we were looking forward to getting help from Terrell Brandon, the All-Star point guard we acquired from the Cavaliers in the Vin Baker trade. He didn't let us down.

The season before, we had ranked near the bottom of the league in assists. With his skill at finding the open man, we became better in that area. In the end, though, we won only three more games—in large part because Terrell sprained his ankle in early February and appeared in just 50 games. If Terrell hadn't been hurt, we might have made the playoffs. Before losing nine in a row in March, we were a respectable 29-29. It didn't help that Glenn, our top scorer, and Tyrone Hill, our top rebounder, who we also got in the Baker deal, missed a bunch of games as well.

Nonetheless, someone had to go. That someone turned out to be, as it often is in these situations, our coach.

I felt bad for Chris, despite how tough he was on me early on. He had been given just two years to turn around a franchise that hadn't reached the postseason since 1991. As soon as I heard the news, I thought to myself, *The NBA sure is cutthroat.* I had never seen anyone fired before, from anything.

The new coach would be George Karl, who had parted ways with the Seattle Sonics a couple of months before. He was the man I wanted from the moment I learned Chris was out.

The Sonics won at least 55 games in each of his six full seasons. Only the Bulls, which beat them in six games in the 1996 Finals, won more during that stretch. George had apparently gotten on the wrong side of the owner, Barry Ackerley, and the general manager, Wally Walker. So what? Frankly, it's a wonder coaches and the people above them coexist as long as they do. I felt so strongly about George that I flew to DC to make the case in person to Senator Kohl.

Meeting with the senator was memorable, it being my first visit to the Capitol building. He and I had gotten along wonderfully from the beginning. As a matter of fact, whenever he was in Milwaukee, we met for lunch at a hotel downtown. I was 100 percent honest with him about any issues with the team, and he appreciated that.

No, he wasn't an expert in the nuances and subtleties of the game but being such an astute businessman and politician, he surrounded himself with the best people and always asked the appropriate questions. That's why it always seemed odd to me whenever other players in the league saw their owner as the enemy. I never felt that way about Senator Kohl.

I told him George was the coach we needed if we were serious about becoming one of the elite teams. The senator didn't say much, although I got the impression that George's name had come up before. I was certain that, if we didn't hire him, someone else would.

Shortly afterward, George was brought on, and I couldn't wait to work with him. Except I would have to.

In the summer of 1998, the players and owners were at war once again, and no one would get on the court until it was resolved. The conflict was over the almighty dollar—is there ever anything else?—the owners trying to increase their share of the basketball-related income (gate receipts, broadcast rights, etc.), the players trying to keep their share at the current level.

It was more complicated than that, obviously, but when July 1 arrived and there was still no clear end in sight, the owners imposed a lockout. They were waging another war, for public opinion, which they won without much trouble. They cast us as the bad guys, knowing that fans wouldn't see any difference between a strike and a lockout. We came to the arena one day to show people we were ready to get to work, that it was the owners who were keeping us out.

Some good that did. If only social media had been around back then. We could have taken our case directly to the fans, instead of relying on the mainstream press. I have no doubt we would have received a lot more support. Did racism play a role? How could it not? When owners, who are white, seek more money, they are "shrewd." When players, who are predominantly black, seek more money, they are "greedy." Words tell you a lot.

While both sides stubbornly dug in, fall turning into winter, I remained in Connecticut, working out with my college buddies Donny Marshall and Kevin Ollie. It felt like old times.

Finally, in January 1999, the two sides reached an agreement. The season was cut to 50 games, with every team forced to play on a number of back-to-back-to-back nights. I can't overstate how tiring that is, especially for the older players. Hey, at least we would have a season, and before I knew it I was back in Milwaukee. So much about the place would be the same: the sense of isolation, the snow, the Bucks overshadowed by Brett Favre and the Packers.

But there was hope. The George Karl era—when drama, on and off the court, was something you could count on—was about to get under way.

Say what you want about the man. He was never boring.

JESUS AND GEORGE

Come to think of it, I was used to a little drama of my own by the time George took over, mine taking place in reel—not real—life.

It began in January 1997, when we played the Knicks in New York. Allan Houston, one of the best shooting guards in the game, was having a strong first half at my expense. I was usually successful at tuning out any comments from the fans sitting in the courtside seats, but one comment got through loud and clear:

"Are you going to guard Allan tonight?" some wiseguy yelled.

The voice belonged to film director Spike Lee (*Do the*

Right Thing, Jungle Fever), a die-hard Knicks fan. Even if you've never seen a Spike Lee film, if you've watched a Knicks game on television, you know who I'm talking about. Whenever the official makes a questionable call against the Knicks, the camera will go right to Spike, wearing a team jersey, giving the guy more abuse than the coaches do.

I didn't say a word. Start responding to hecklers, playful or not, and you'll never stop.

A few months later, on our next visit to the Garden, Spike kept trying to get my attention, but I kept ignoring him. Allan was playing well again, and Spike, I figured, would give me another hard time.

At halftime, he finally walked over to me.

"I'm doing a film and I want to know if you'd be interested in coming to New York to audition for it," he said. Not what I expected to hear.

I was interested, of course, but I didn't get too excited. Spike planned to audition a number of players he'd run into at the Garden.

In April, a few days after the season ended, I went to New York to give it a shot. That was the only upside of us missing the playoffs. If we had made it, I wouldn't have been able to try out for two weeks, maybe longer. Spike couldn't wait forever. I wasn't Marlon Brando.

I would be auditioning to play Jesus Shuttlesworth, a high school basketball phenom who has to choose which college scholarship to accept. Remind you of anyone?

His story, however, was more complicated. His father was in prison for accidentally killing his wife, though he would now have a chance to get his sentence reduced if Jesus were to pick the governor's alma mater.

For once, I didn't do any preparation. There was no point. I had no concept of what this Jesus guy was supposed to be like. So I read with a couple of different actresses. We did a love scene—we went over lines, that's it, I swear—and I was out of there. Good thing I had no plans to give up my day job.

I must have done well enough, because Spike asked me to return a week later for a second audition, and then a third. For the third, he asked Denzel Washington, who had already signed on to play Jesus's father, to read with me. Having been in the league for a year by this point, I was used to meeting people who were accomplished in their fields.

Meeting Denzel was different. I was in awe.

Denzel, a huge Lakers fan, put me at ease right away. He didn't act as if he was the star and everybody else was there to serve his needs. I can think of some people I've come across who could learn a lesson from him. I felt chemistry between the two of us, as did Spike. He called a day or two later.

"Do you think you can commit to this?" he asked.

Good question. I had worked as hard as I could for seven straight months, since training camp began, and I needed a break, mentally and physically. Instead, I would now have to take on another tough job, one I'd be doing for the first time. There would go my summer.

I shared those reservations with Shannon, who, as usual, knocked some sense into me.

"Who cares about your summer?" she said. "Do you know how many people would sell their souls to the devil to be in a Spike Lee film?"

It helped when Spike said he would set me up with an apartment in the city and I found a gym at Chelsea Piers to work out every day after we finished on the set. He also told me that I would get my share of days off. It was an offer, to quote Brando from *The Godfather*, I couldn't refuse. If I did, I knew I would regret the decision for the rest of my life.

He Got Game, released in the spring of 1998, was an experience I will always cherish, not merely for a chance to be around Spike, Denzel, and dozens of other talented artists but also for the message it sends to young people in every walk of life: you can achieve your goals as long as you stay true to yourself.

I also found out that I could show my emotions, and it was okay; life would go on. I had become quite an expert at keeping my guard up, from having been around parents who weren't very affectionate and kids who made it clear I wasn't one of them. Believe it or not, I couldn't even tell somebody I cared about that I missed them. It was not until I began working on the film, trying to get my character to open up, that it hit me: I need to learn how to tell other people how I feel about them.

Coming to the rescue was Susan Batson, my acting coach, who worked with me day after day for six weeks.

Any time we dealt with a character Jesus encounters in the script, Susan asked me to compare that person to somebody I knew. If I was supposed to be mad at Denzel, she'd have me reflect on times when I was mad at my real father. I felt like I was in therapy.

"The audience needs to understand what you're feeling and thinking, and see it on your face," Susan explained.

Before every scene, I glanced at the notes I'd jotted down in a log.

What helped me tremendously was that I could relate to the responsibilities that Jesus was dealing with. It was up to him to watch over his younger sister, as it had been up to Rosalind and me, with help from Mom, to watch over Tierra. Most kids that age couldn't begin to imagine what it would feel like to be responsible for another human being. They have enough trouble trying to keep themselves in line.

Preparing for each day of filming was no different from preparing for a game. Eat the right foods, get enough sleep, and limit the distractions. And, of course, know your lines!

I didn't look at any scenes, or "dailies," as they are known in the biz, while we were still shooting, though Spike did, and liked what I was giving him. It was not until I was in Los Angeles months later that I sat down in a screening room and watched the finished product for the first time. I have never enjoyed looking at myself on the screen, even the highlights on *SportsCenter*, and I felt just as uneasy this time, although I was impressed by the job Spike did. Not a single moment seemed inauthentic.

Looking back, I remember thinking how dysfunctional Jesus's family was, but as I have gotten older, I see things differently. Teammates complained to me constantly: "My family is so messed up."

"Dude," I'd tell them, "everyone's family has problems."

What *He Got Game* also showed me is the importance of being a leader in your own family, and whether you are the parent or the child, you always have an opportunity to stand up for what is right. It doesn't mean others will always follow you. And, by taking a stand, you might put up barriers that will not be easy to break through. But if you stand for nothing, you will fall for anything.

With the lockout finally over, I was eager to get back on the court. Having more time off than normal was a welcome change, but the career of an NBA player is short enough, and there was so much I wanted to accomplish. You could say the same about George Karl. He was as demanding as anyone I've ever known in the game—in any endeavor, really. He made Jim Calhoun seem almost laid-back.

From day 1, there was a structure under George that we hadn't seen before. Everyone, from the starters to the last man on the bench, was held accountable. Rookies were required to be at the facility for workouts and lifts before practice. More than any coach I played for, George involved every man in the offense. That kept players engaged for the whole 48 minutes, knowing that, at any moment, Coach might call a play for you.

One play George drew up was called "the Hammer," after Darvin Ham, a backup forward. You still see it in the NBA today. Darvin would catch the ball on the block, spin toward the baseline, and then find me in the opposite corner for a three. I would get credit for the bucket, but the play was made by Darvin.

"Just because I call your number," George told us, "does not mean it's time for you to score; it means it's your time to make a play for the team."

Every play has a wide variety of options, the idea being to find the best option, whether it's a mismatch or a blown assignment by the defense. Fail to do that, and your chances of scoring on that possession go down.

George taught me to see the entire game. When we went over film in the locker room, he explained precisely what I did wrong and what I needed to do better the next time. It seems obvious, I know, but you would be amazed at how many coaches force players to watch hours of tape without helping them see their mistakes.

Nor was George hesitant to bring in other experts to help out, like Gerald Oliver, a friend from his days in the Continental Basketball Association (CBA), pro basketball's minor leagues.

G.O., as we called Oliver, was a good ol' country boy who knew as much about shooting as anyone I'd ever met. If learning from the coaches in California and Karl Hobbs at UConn was the equivalent of an undergraduate seminar in Shooting 101, G.O. was where I went to earn my master's. He'd sit 20 rows up in the stands, or higher, when I was on the court alone, practicing my shot a couple of hours before tip-off. Lots of times I didn't know he was there. He taught me how imperative it was to reach the same level every time—meaning, how high I was off the ground when the ball left my hand.

I tried to reach that level, game after game, year after year. I didn't always achieve it. Your legs get fatigued, and the same commitment you had in the first quarter may not be there in the fourth. Fortunately, more often than not, I got there—and stayed there—when it mattered most. Like Game 6 against the Spurs.

"Let me tell ya something, buddy," G.O. said on more than a few occasions. "I didn't watch whether the ball went through, but you're going to have a good game tonight. I watched your lift, and you were consistent the whole time."

More important, I learned to figure out when I *wasn't* consistent and what adjustments I needed to make.

Eventually, G.O. stopped showing up; he had taught me everything he could, and it was my job to pass the knowledge on to others.

We got off to a good start in the shortened 1998–1999 season, taking five of our first six, three of the wins coming on the road.

Then, in early March, we won six in a row, including victories over the Bulls, Knicks, and Sonics, in one of the dreaded back-to-back-to-backs. Being just 23 years old, I wasn't as bothered by playing for three straight nights as much as some of the veterans, and with Terrell back in sync, I was scoring my share of points.

I was also scoring at the bargaining table.

As a member of the National Basketball Players Association's executive committee, I sat in on every meeting during the lockout, learning a great deal about the business side of the game. So when I met with the senator to seek a contract extension, I didn't bring an agent. Under the new agreement, there was a maximum salary a third-year player could make. What would be the point of handing over 4 percent of that amount to an agent?

Of course, I still needed an attorney to read the contract. I hired Johnnie Cochran, who you might have heard of; he defended O. J. Simpson in his 1995 double-murder trial. Man, did Johnnie know how to take over a room, and a jury, as we know. The extension was for six years and $70.9 million. I never played the game for money, but it was nice to be rewarded for the hard work.

The same went for the team itself. For the first time since I entered the league in '96, we featured the right blend of scoring, rebounding, and defense. There seemed no need to change a thing.

But on March 11, we dealt Terrell Brandon, Tyrone Hill, and Elliot Perry, in a three-team trade involving New Jersey and Minnesota.

The biggest prize we received in return was point guard Sam Cassell. As talented as Terrell was—in a 1997 cover story, *Sports Illustrated* called him the best point guard in the NBA—I guess that wasn't enough for George. He preferred fiery, take-charge individuals. Like himself.

Sam, who played a key role on the Houston Rockets squads that won back-to-back titles in the mid-1990s, was that, and much more. He was not hesitant to give it right back to George whenever he got on his case. What I didn't realize back then was that George was more in love with the players in the league he didn't have than the players he did.

Sam, coming off an injury, needed some time to round into shape, but when he did, he helped us finish the season at 28-22 to gain the No. 7 seed in the Eastern Conference.

We were going to the playoffs. At last.

Too bad we didn't stick around for long, losing three straight to the Indiana Pacers, one on a tip-in with less than a second to go in OT. Regardless, we learned a great deal from just being in games in which something larger was at stake. The fans in Milwaukee were excited about the future.

The next year, after going 42-40, we met Indiana again in the opening round, and lost again.

At least we made it a series this time, falling in five, and by only one point in the deciding game. George was frustrated, and with good reason. When you invest that much effort, it hurts more than you can imagine. But there was no shame in losing to Indiana, who would go on to the Finals that season, falling to the Lakers in six. The Pacers were loaded: Rik Smits, Jalen Rose, Dale Davis, and the premier shooter in the game, Reggie Miller.

Reggie, who scored 41 points in Game 5 of our series—18 in the final quarter!—was a nightmare cover for me. He ran off screens, and grabbed you, and threw you in one direction while he took off in the other. I could not stay in front of him.

Once, as we waited for a jump ball, I looked at his shoes, which were very similar to mine, except he had his name on them. I thought that was the coolest thing.

"How did you get those?" I asked.

"Ten years," he said, signaling a rite of passage.

Got it, Reg.

In the summer of 2000, I had another performance to prepare for. This one would be in Sydney, Australia, where I would play for my country in the Olympics.

I was as big a fan as anybody of the original dream team in 1992, with Magic, Michael, and Larry, never imagining it could be me out there. Until the week of the 1996 Games in Atlanta. I was working out at the facility in Storrs, getting ready for my rookie year in the league, when someone from the university said to me: "In four years, you will be playing in the Olympics."

I let that sink in for a moment, and I liked the way it sounded. At the same time I thought, *let's not get ahead of ourselves. I haven't played my first game in the NBA yet!*

When 2000 rolled around and I made the team, I couldn't have been more pumped.

What a team it was: Alonzo Mourning, Tim Hardaway, Jason Kidd, Vince Carter, Antonio McDyess, Gary Payton, Shareef Abdur-Rahim, Vin Baker, Allan Houston, Steve Smith, and my buddy from South Carolina, Kevin Garnett.

Like the 1992 and 1996 squads, we were supposed to crush everyone we played. Try telling that to the proud men who represented Lithuania, who had a few dreams of their own.

We beat them by only nine points in our third game, and I say "only" because, prior to that, no opponent had come closer than 22 points against a US team in the Olympics since we began to use professionals in 1992. We even trailed, by a point, with a little under 18 minutes to go. Never had the United States been behind in the second half.

That was nothing compared to what happened when we played Lithuania a second time, in the semis. The pressure was unlike anything I had ever experienced, and Rudy Tomjanovich, our coach, apparently felt it, as well. Late in the game, we needed stops more than baskets, but when Mourning, our center, fouled out, Rudy T. signaled for me to go in.

Tim Hardaway couldn't contain himself. "Why are you putting Ray Allen in when we need rebounding?" he shouted. Rudy T. recognized his error, thank goodness, and sent for the six-foot-nine McDyess instead.

It didn't help that the whole continent seemed to be against us. In a pre-Olympics tune-up against Australia's national team, Vince Carter and Andrew Gaze, one of their heroes, got into a tussle in the early going. As he fell to the floor, Gaze pulled Vince down with him. Vince was irate. He got up and tried to step over Gaze but accidentally stepped *on* him. The fans thought it was no accident.

From then on, we were the nasty Americans. They booed us and threw junk onto the court . . . and Australia was one of our allies!

Anyway, when we got to the final seconds of the second Lithuania game, we were in real trouble. Down by only two, Sarunas Jasikevicius, who had burned us for 27 points already, launched a three from 22 feet. It goes in, we lose. Let me repeat: we lose.

I don't have to tell you he missed. The shot would be that historic.

Two days later, we captured the gold against France, 85–75, Vince and I both scoring 13 points. I cherish that gold medal, and I don't even want to think how I'd feel today if that ball had gone in.

Going into the 2000–01 season, my fifth, the expectations were high. For one thing, we couldn't have had a more capable floor general than Sam Cassell. Sam played with a lot of energy, and his mouth was always going as well. He cracked me up with the stories he told, calling me "RayAllen," as if my name was one word. You need guys like Sam. The NBA season can be a grind, and although you should focus on what you're trying to accomplish, you must never forget it's a game.

Sam, having been around longer than the rest of us, knew how to remain calm. When we started the year 3-9,

George was beside himself. He complained to the press we were spoiled brats and millionaire babies.

But Sam was sure we weren't as bad as our record; we simply had the misfortune of catching hot teams at the worst time.

"You need to chill the fuck out," he told George. "You are panicking. The season has barely begun."

George thought he scared us with his comments to the reporters. He didn't. He made us angry, with him, and you never want to get players angry with their coach. Once you go down that path, there is no guarantee you can ever go back.

Sam was right. We weren't as bad as our record. From late November through the end of December, we won 13 of 17. One of those wins came against Shaq, Kobe, and the Lakers, the defending champs, in Los Angeles. Joel Przybilla, our seven-foot-one rookie center, wasn't afraid of Shaq. Without any help, he made him alter his shots. There were centers who had been in the league for years who couldn't do that.

We were just getting started.

In January, we won eight in a row, and finished 52-30 to claim our first division crown since 1986, and the number 2 seed in the East behind the Philadelphia 76ers. After knocking off the Orlando Magic, three games to one, in the opening round, and taking the first two from the Charlotte Hornets, a trip to the conference finals seemed inevitable. But the Hornets held serve to even the series and upset us in Game 5, 94–86, to assume a 3–2 lead. It was now up to the so-called Big Three of Glenn, Sam, and myself to keep our season alive, and that's what we did, winning Game 6 in Charlotte, 104–97. Sam led the way with 33 points and

11 assists; Glenn added 29, and I had 23. We went on to capture Game 7, 104–95. On to Philadelphia.

I was excited, and not because I'd get another crack at Iverson. I was excited to have a crack at winning it all, especially after never advancing past the Elite Eight at UConn. I'd won a championship before, in high school, but that was one state out of 50. Winning a title at this level would mean we were the best team in the world.

The Sixers would present quite a challenge. In addition to Iverson, the league MVP, they had Dikembe Mutombo, the Defensive Player of the Year; Aaron McKie, the Sixth Man of the Year; and a very good point guard, Eric Snow.

In Philly, we did what we set out to do, splitting the first two games to seize the home court. Unfortunately, we gave it back to them in Game 4, falling by six, when we had an opportunity to go up 3–1.

Then, in Game 5, after McKie was way short on two free throws with 13.9 seconds remaining, it came down to our final possession, the Sixers leading, 89–88.

Time-out's called.

The last time I was in a similar situation, against a team with Allen Iverson, Coach Calhoun put his faith in me and we won the game.

This time George designed a play for Glenn, and it made all the sense in the world; he was a phenomenal scorer.

The ball was inbounded to Sam, who dribbled for a while before passing it to Glenn. With McKie on him, Glenn maneuvered into a good position on the baseline and threw it up from 10 feet. He doesn't miss that shot.

He missed *that* shot.

I got a hand on the ball and tried to tip it in, but I didn't come close. Game over.

The series, thank goodness, was not.

Two days later, we won Game 6 at home 110–100. I had a career night: 41 points, hitting nine of 13 threes, and going on a 19-0 run of my own in the first half. Now tied at three games apiece, we felt confident we could take the deciding game on their floor. We had won there once and could easily have won twice.

Then, on Saturday, we received the news that changed everything.

The day before, in Game 6, Iverson was driving down the lane when Scott Williams, our power forward, elbowed him in the chin.

Iverson fell to the floor. A hard foul, without question, but it wasn't a dirty play. Scott was trying to get his hand on his hip, but with Iverson being low to the ground, it caught his chin instead.

Way to go, Scott, we thought. Way to let the little guy know he can't barrel his way into the paint and expect to get out unscathed. Besides, the refs didn't see anything out of the ordinary, and Scott went on to score 12 big points for us. He was one of those guys, whenever he took a jump shot, you shouted: "No, no, no, no . . . great shot!"

The league saw it differently, upgrading the foul on Saturday to a "flagrant foul penalty 2." Bottom line: the league suspended Scott for Game 7 because he had racked up too many penalty points in the playoffs, with flagrants also against Orlando and Charlotte.

When we got word of this, shortly after landing in Philadelphia, we were outraged. It wasn't as if the foul affected the outcome of the game; Iverson got up and was his usual pesky, disruptive self. But by suspending Scott, the NBA was, quite possibly, affecting the outcome of a whole series, and you're talking about a game that could forever shape people's lives, on both sides.

So why would the league do that?

I have a theory, which I put forward at the time and received a lot of heat for, but I still believe it today: the league suspended Scott because it wanted us to lose.

Or to put it another way: the league wanted the Sixers to win.

Go back to June 2001, imagine you work for the NBA, and ask yourself: Who would generate higher ratings, and more revenue, in the Finals against the Lakers? Allen Iverson and company from a franchise as steeped in history as the Philadelphia 76ers, where Wilt and Dr. J were legends?

Or a cast of unknowns from Wisconsin, the Cheese State?

For the record, I'm not the type who believes in conspiracy theories. Just this one. Need more proof? The Sixers attempted 66 more free throws than we did, almost 10 more per game, and committed nine fewer technicals.

I rest my case.

Scott got a lot of rebounds, but more than that, he was an emotional leader, and not having him on the bench—when you are suspended, you can't be in the building—was as much of a blow as not having him on the floor.

Still, we had to let go of our anger, and quickly. Game 7 was here, and you never know if an opportunity like this will come again. Dan Marino, the star Miami Dolphins quarterback, was only 23 years old in 1985 when he played in his first Super Bowl. He didn't play in another.

We kept the game close, down by six at the half. Then, with about five minutes to go in the third quarter, I collided with Eric Snow while driving to the basket and bruised my left knee. I had to come out. We were down seven at the time, and when I came back with 10 minutes to go in the fourth, the lead was 14. The final: Sixers 108, Bucks 91.

Iverson dominated with 44 points, while Mutombo finished with 23 points, 19 boards, and seven blocks. You can't tell me Scott Williams wouldn't have made a difference, as Philly outrebounded us, 47 to 38.

The mood in the locker room was as somber as you'd expect. Even Sam didn't have much to say. The shame of it was that we matched up extremely well against the Lakers, beating them both times in the regular season, and no doubt we would have given them a more competitive series than the Sixers, who lost four in a row after taking the opener. I couldn't bear to watch one minute of the Finals. That should have been us out there.

Over the next couple of weeks, as the disappointment began to subside, I took a broader view of what we accomplished. The future could not be brighter.

Sam, at 31, was getting up there a bit, but Glenn and I were still in our twenties, and Tim Thomas, 24, was on the verge of breaking through. Then there was George Karl, as intelligent and innovative as any coach in the NBA, who'd taken us to the playoffs three straight years. He got us to believe in ourselves, and that's not as easy as it sounds.

What could possibly go wrong?

9

THE BUCK STOPS HERE

When you win 52 games and come close to reaching the Finals, you don't let any warning signs get you down.

One sign came in an article *Sports Illustrated* did on me in February 2001, the biggest, to that point, of my career. The earlier stories, though positive, had been in the local paper.

But in the *SI* piece, I was taken to task for the way I carried myself . . . by my own coach! I could not believe it, and for the first time I wondered: Is this guy really on my side?

"I call him Barbie Doll because he wants to be pretty," George told the writer. "He's a great player, but he cares too much about having style, making highlights, and being cool. Basketball isn't about being cool. It's a tough, competitive game and to win, you have to be mean, you have to be an assassin, and that's not Ray."

George, apparently, thought I should have been more upset after two recent games in which the guy I was guarding had a big night. First of all, those guys were great players; they had big nights against everyone. Besides, like any professional, I had a lot of pride, so, of course, I was upset; I just didn't show it the way others did.

He got on my case, get this, for smiling.

"Two guys drop 84 points on your ass," George said, "and I'm thinking, 'Where's the pissed-off competitor?' I look at Ray, he's out there smiling. Tell me what that's all about."

I'll tell you exactly what that was about. I smiled because I was able to do something I loved for a living, even when it didn't go my way. Shannon was right when I poured my soul out to her on the pier the night of the draft: I was blessed.

George even got upset with me for smiling during practice. Once, after he caught Sam and me laughing, he quickly pulled me aside.

"I can't have my best player messing around on the sideline," he said. "We're trying to be serious, and the other guys are following you."

Frankly, I didn't see anything wrong with playing the game with joy. I don't believe smiling held Magic Johnson back. Besides, if you practice hard, what difference should it make whether you play with anger or not? Anger is not going to help you set a solid screen or throw an accurate pass or box out your man. If anything, anger will take you out of your rhythm.

George's suggestion that I cared too much about being "cool" didn't make sense to me either. Whenever I floated in the air and laid the ball in softly off the glass, people would tell me: "Man, that looked so smooth."

That's because it wasn't an aggressive move, and it didn't have to be. I never saw the upside in using more energy than you needed to. Make the other guy spend it. Come the fourth quarter, you'll have the fresher legs.

He was also hard on me in front of my teammates. At least I knew it was coming.

"There are going to be times when I got to get on you to use you as an example so I can get on the other guys," George said. "They'll see that I am not playing favorites. You're going to have to roll with it."

Which I did, over and over. But getting on me in public, as he did in the *Sports Illustrated* interview, was entirely different. That I would *not* roll with.

Another warning sign was when I called Terry Stotts, one of our assistant coaches, in the summer of 2001 to see if he wanted to join me for a round of golf at the country club I belonged to. Terry and I teed it up as often as we could.

"George said I can't play golf with you," he said.

He told you what? How my playing golf with Terry had anything to do with the fortunes of the Milwaukee Bucks was beyond me.

Terry was doing what he was told. With George, you were either with him or against him, and the other coaches couldn't afford to be against him.

So when did everything we built over three years begin to unravel? When we signed Anthony Mason.

I was excited when we picked up Anthony, a free agent,

a week before the start of the 2001–02 season. The one ingredient we lacked was toughness, and Anthony would give us that, as he gave it to the Knicks as a power forward in the mid-1990s, when they almost won the championship, and to the Heat, where he was an All-Star in 2001. Plus, Anthony, may he rest in peace, was a good man and always kind to me.

That fall, with him averaging 7.5 rebounds, we took nine of our first 10.

But then we hit the road—and the skids. We lost five in a row, four by double digits. Although we seemed to turn things around in January, when we won eight straight, that run was misleading. Our chemistry was rotten under the surface, so it was no surprise when we dropped 27 of the next 40. You can't hide your flaws for long. Not on a stage this big.

The problem was Anthony. Instead of searching for ways to fit in as the new guy, he expected everybody else to conform to him.

Bill Bradley, the former Knick, put it best in his book *Life on the Run,* where he describes the sacrifices required from every player to win a title: "A team championship exposes the limits of self-reliance, selfishness, and irresponsibility. One man alone can't make it happen; in fact, the contrary is true: a single man can prevent it from happening."

Bradley wrote that in 1976, and as much as basketball has changed, that's one truth about the sport that hasn't.

Anthony wanted the ball on almost every possession, and when we did not give it to him, he complained to no end and didn't care who might notice. A lot of times, when I took a three in transition, he lowered his hands and headed down the court with the worst body language you could imagine, as if I had thrown the ball into Lake Michigan. Our style was playing fast and taking the first good shot we saw. But with him holding on to the ball in the post—for an eternity, it seemed—we went from shooting with 16 or 18 seconds left on the 24-second clock to shooting with three or four seconds. He disrupted our whole continuity.

The huddles were the worst. George would be giving instructions when Anthony would turn his chair to the side and look into the crowd. He didn't listen to a word George said. I had never seen a player act like that, not even in junior high. He wasn't just disrespecting the coach; he was disrespecting the game and his teammates. There were times Sam would go to the baseline to bring the ball up after a made basket, which was his job as point guard, and Anthony would rush down there to beat him to it. Good luck getting the ball out of his hands.

You had to assume George, with his need to always be in control, would make sure to keep Anthony in line. Oh, he tried, for a while, but Anthony would give it right back to him: "You fat motherfucker, shut the fuck up."

Normally, when a player doesn't respect the coach, he's benched, and if that doesn't set him straight, he's fined. The last resort is to waive the guy, and it doesn't matter how much money he is making or what holes it will create for the roster.

George didn't take any of those steps. He was afraid of Anthony. He let him get away with anything.

My teammates and I had nothing to be proud of either. We didn't try to confront Anthony, as individuals or as a unit. We tried to please him so he wouldn't be angry with us. Perhaps we were also afraid of him.

We should have seen it coming. Others around the league

did. After a game against the Heat, one of their guys stopped by to visit us in the locker room.

"Why didn't you call me?" said the player, who had been Anthony's teammate for several years and was familiar with his antics. "I would have told you."

"Thanks a lot," I said. "Now you tell me."

Actually, this player wasn't the first. One day in training camp, before we signed Anthony, Ervin Johnson, our center, gave me a call:

"Ray, be careful what you wish for," Ervin said. "He wants that ball, and he can destroy everything that's going on."

I went to our general manager, Ernie Grunfeld, to see if he could solve the problem. Ernie reached out to a few teams, but nobody wanted Anthony.

"You have to assume this is what we're going to have for the rest of the year," he told me.

We would also have George, who didn't know how to avoid controversy. I'm no psychologist, but it was almost as if he went looking for it.

Take the comments he made in an interview with *Esquire*, which hit the newsstands in March of that season. The reporter asked about Doc Rivers, who was coaching the Orlando Magic. Easy enough. Just say a few kind words, and go on to the next question.

Except nothing was easy for George. He indicated that Doc, who went directly from the TV booth to the Orlando job, hadn't paid his dues as an assistant coach in the NBA, that he had been "anointed," and that it would result in "four or five more anointments of the young Afro-American coach."

What George said was racist, and there was no getting around it. What about Larry Bird? He had not been an assistant coach either, before he was hired by the Pacers in 1997. George didn't bring his name up. By the way, Doc played in the league for 13 years. Don't tell me that's not paying your dues.

My teammates and I didn't confront George, as we didn't confront Anthony. We talked to the media when we should have talked to him.

Between Anthony and George, you can see how distracted we were, and, ultimately, why the losses piled up.

Still, heading into the final game of the regular season, a win over the Pistons in Detroit would put us in the playoffs and then, who knows? We certainly had the talent to make a nice run.

Some players embraced the challenge, like Darvin Ham, who entered the locker room wearing his military fatigues.

Some didn't, including me. I told Shannon I didn't want to make the playoffs. It sounds awful, I know, but let me explain. Making the playoffs, in my opinion, would've made everything that went wrong that season okay, and it was anything but okay. It was despicable, and I was sure the same squabbles would sabotage us again, this time before a national audience. I wanted no part of that.

There was nothing to worry about. The Pistons led by 20 at the half and didn't look back. The final: 123 to 89. I scored six points in 23 minutes.

From nearly reaching the Finals to being in the draft lottery with the other losers, ladies and gentlemen, these are your Milwaukee Bucks. And that's life in the NBA—no guarantees from one year to the next.

Now what? If no one wanted Anthony, who would go? Somebody had to. You don't fall apart as fast as we did and stand pat. Not if you're George or Ernie and you hope to keep your own job.

In August, we got the answer: Glenn Robinson. The Bucks sent Glenn to the Hawks for Toni Kukoc, Leon Smith, and a first-round draft choice in 2003.

Good move, I thought. Tim Thomas could definitely fill his place. I actually felt he had the potential to be the best player in the league. Besides being a tremendous shooter, Tim could handle the ball and was extremely athletic. He was six-foot-ten and could play every position on the floor, including point guard.

If only I had kept my opinions to myself. Instead, at camp that fall, I criticized Glenn for how he dealt with an ankle injury, and when he found out, he left me a nasty message through a friend of mine. I didn't blame him. Glenn and I won a lot of games together, and he was one of the best I ever played with. That's what I should have told the reporters. Later on, when I experienced my own ankle problems, I felt even worse. I understood pain in a way I never had before.

Glenn was not the only one to go. George also fired a few of the assistant coaches, including Terry Stotts, who had been with him for many years.

No way did Terry deserve it, and we suspected it was only because George was afraid the senator would ask him to take over if the team continued to struggle. Terry did a good job on the occasions he filled in for George. He was composed on the sidelines—imagine that—which helped us compete with a looseness you didn't see otherwise.

But parting with Glenn and the coaches didn't turn things around. We won a few, then lost a few, never showing signs of the team that made it to the Eastern Conference finals only two seasons before. By the end of January, we were barely over .500, and as you might guess, my relationship with George became more tenuous than ever. He was now questioning how tough I was.

When our trainer told me not to practice one day because of the tendonitis in my knee, George saw his opening.

"George isn't happy with you," the reporters said.

"I don't know what you're talking about," I replied.

Soon enough, I found out. George, without saying a word to me first—nothing unusual there—had gotten on my case for not practicing, with no mention of what the trainer advised. You can find fault with me, but not with my willingness to practice or to play in pain. When I got to the NBA my goal was to be like Cal Ripken Jr., the Hall of Fame infielder for the Baltimore Orioles, who didn't miss a game for more than 16 years. I wasn't sure how good I'd become, but I'd show up every day.

Fortunately, I was able to avoid serious injuries and do just that. Not until my sixth season, after appearing in 400 straight games, did I miss my first.

I was sitting on the training table before our game against the Houston Rockets in December 2001 when tendonitis flared up. I jumped up and down. I practically sprinted in the hallway. I tried everything I could think of to get loose, to no avail; my leg was too sore. I felt awful for the people who had come to see me for the first time.

In any case, I allowed George to get to me, and that was my fault, not his. From then on, whenever I twisted my ankle in a game or in practice, I forced myself back on the court regardless of how severely it was hurting. I refused to let anyone think for one second that George was right about me.

Yet, no matter what I did, he found a way to make me wrong. Back in 2000, I was with several executives at the Nike Factory Store in Portland one day, checking out the latest sneakers, when we bumped into him.

"Hey, how's it going, George?" they said.

There was no hello or warm response of any kind.

"Why you hanging around with this guy?" he said. "You should have seen the high school play he made last night."

George walked away and did not say another word. Keep in mind, I had scored 35 that same evening against the Clippers, on 14 of 19 from the field, in a game we won, 104–85. George didn't bring that up, no. Instead, he felt the need to put me down in front of others.

He never displayed the slightest emotion whenever we went on a big run and the other team had to call a time-out. Other coaches clap or pump their fist whenever that happens. Not him. The joint would be going nuts, and he would stand there as if we were down 20 points instead of up 20.

Later in my career, with Nate McMillan or Bob Hill or Doc Rivers, I found it odd to be with coaches who cheered us on. I hadn't seen that kind of passion on the bench since Coach Calhoun.

George once told me: "Sometimes, Ray, you just need to be a dumb basketball player."

Translation: do what I tell you to do, and stop asking so many damn questions!

I could never figure out why George would say something like that. I would think that, if anything, a coach would want to seek out smart players who ask a lot of questions. Asking questions, it stands to reason, would make you more prepared for any surprises on the court.

Years later, I heard from players in Denver what George supposedly told Carmelo Anthony, whom he also had problems with:

"Carmelo, you're a dumb basketball player."

I know Carmelo, and that couldn't be further from the truth.

I have no idea why George disliked me so much. It wasn't that way in the beginning. He lived down the street, and we used to play volleyball in the backyard and have meals together. He invited me to a golf tournament he organized in Boise.

Maybe he was envious of the relationship I had with the senator or maybe he felt I had more power than he did. Another theory is that he wasn't fond of stars. Except for Gary Payton, whom he coached in Seattle and, later, Milwaukee, I can't recall a high-profile player on one of George's teams he *did* get along with.

George once complained to me about his teammate from the 1970s, George Gervin, aka "The Iceman."

Gervin, one of the most explosive scorers the game has ever seen, would take the shot even if he was doubled and the other George was wide open. And with good reason. In his career, mostly with the Spurs, the Iceman shot over 50 percent. George, though, never forgave Gervin for not passing the ball to him, and I really believe he took his resentment out on other stars.

The less regarded players, on the other hand, he'd rave about, such as Mark Pope, our seldom-used forward. That was because George had been one of them.

"He's our best player in practice," he'd tell us. "All you guys need to be like Mark."

If George was so in love with Mark, the rest of us wondered, why the hell wasn't he starting him every night?

Whatever it was that pitted him against me, I didn't realize how dire the situation truly was until I spoke to Sam Mitchell, an assistant coach who joined the Bucks in 2002. I was working out on the first floor at the practice facility when Sam, whose office was on the second floor, saw me and came down.

"Don't trust none of those motherfuckers up there," Sam told me. "I was in a meeting, and every one of them was ripping you. They sat there and tried to convince me you're a problem. 'Problem?' I told them. 'I don't see how he's a problem. He's here every day working on his game.'"

If Sam could see how dedicated I was, I have to believe the other coaches could see it as well. And if they did, how come they did not tell George he was wrong about me? Again, you're either with him or against him.

I received a similar warning from one of my teammates.

"I need to talk to you," he told me one day when I walked into the locker room. "There are a lot of cats in here saying you're not doing this or you're not doing that. I want you to know I see the work you put in."

The locker room is like high school sometimes, with the cliques that form and the gossip, much of it untrue, that somebody spreads. I appreciated that my teammate had the courage to tell me what he'd heard.

Running out of patience, I went to see the senator. If anybody could resolve the issues between George and myself, it was him.

His advice was simple: talk to the man. My response was also simple: too late. Every time I did, George tried to convince me I was angry with Sam or Anthony or Tim, anybody but him.

Senator Kohl, in any case, was not about to tell George what to do. Most owners hand over power to the coaches . . . until the day they let 'em go. I felt I had no choice but to tell the senator that perhaps it would be best for everyone if I were to move on. I wasn't, after all, the type of person to issue an ultimatum. Not that it would have made any difference.

If I could do it over again, I would have reached out to George one final time. My job is to help you win, I would have said, and if you have complaints, come to me instead of the media. I don't appreciate the attacks on my character, and neither does my family.

Why didn't I? Because, growing up with a father in the armed forces, I learned you don't talk back to authority figures. You follow orders. Only years later did I realize that authority figures make terrible choices like the rest of us, and when they do, you need to resist, and hope the people above them listen to what you have to say.

I would've also looked for more support from my teammates. Others, I'm sure, felt the way as the player who warned me did. If we stuck together, we could've forced George to stop playing us off against one another. As I knew from my days at UConn, a team that acts as one is something to behold.

Several weeks after my chat with the senator, the team went on the road. There were about 30 games to go; anything could still happen.

Anything indeed.

I was stretching on the court at the arena in Seattle the day before a game with the Sonics when, every time I turned my back, the cameramen in the tunnel shined their lights on me. I had never seen so many cameras at a practice.

"What's going on?" I asked them.

"There's been a trade," they said.

"Who got traded?"

They pointed at me.

"Say what?"

I went over to gather more information, and as I did, I noticed George walking off the floor at the other end of the court, as if trying to escape. He had known the whole day this deal was in the works, yet he hadn't said a word to me, either on the bus ride from the hotel or once we arrived at the arena. The Bucks were acquiring Gary Payton, one of the premier guards in the game, and swingman Desmond Mason. George told the senator that Michael Redd, my backup, could do everything I did. The senator believed him.

I was shocked. All the speculation leading up to the trade deadline was that Tim Thomas, nearing the end of his contract, was the one on the block, not me. Reporters even asked me what I thought Tim must be going through. Traded or not, I said, he would still get paid. It wasn't as if he'd be sent to prison.

Everything happened quickly from that point on. I went back to the hotel with Kevin Ollie, my buddy from Connecticut, who was also going to the Sonics.

An hour or so later, Nate McMillan, the Seattle coach, picked KO and me up and drove us to meet Howard Schultz, the owner and former CEO of Starbucks, at his house. House? The place was more like a mountain. You didn't know where it began and where it ended.

Howard offered us some coffee. Of course he did. He

told us he had a five-year plan to win the championship, and the Sonics were currently in year two. I loved what he was saying, in one sense: you always want to play for an owner who reaches for the stars. In another, though, I found it almost laughable. You can't put a timetable on winning the title. There are too many unknowns.

My emotions were mixed. I was relieved to be getting away from such a toxic environment, where I had to look over my shoulder every five seconds to find out what George might be saying about me to the media.

On the other hand, I'd grown quite fond of Milwaukee. I'd put everything I had into the franchise, and we had begun to build something special, until, the very next season, it fell apart. We could have won a title, maybe two.

Likewise, George should have been given his due for being an excellent teacher and strategist. He could've created a dynasty wherever he coached. If he hadn't gotten in his own way.

More than anything, I was upset with how the trade went down. If George didn't have the guts to give me a heads-up, Ernie, or the senator, should have done it. A player should never receive news like that from the media.

By the way, I didn't speak to George before I left and haven't spoken to him since. The afternoon of the trade, before KO and I went to meet Howard, I was riding up in the escalator at the hotel while George was riding down. He couldn't make eye contact. That's when I knew it was him who got rid of me.

The deal, if I can be objective for a moment, was a disaster for the Bucks. Payton, a free agent, signed with the Lakers after appearing in just 28 games for Milwaukee, which was knocked out in the first round of the playoffs by the New Jersey Nets. The players I spoke to around the league couldn't figure out what the Bucks were thinking.

"That's bullshit," Shaq told me before my debut as a Sonic, in Los Angeles.

It didn't improve my mood any when, the following night, during my first game at KeyArena, the fans who worshiped Payton held up signs to show how they felt about the deal.

One sign read: FEBRUARY 20, 2003, THE DAY THE SONICS DIED. Ouch.

I was booed when the trade was announced in Milwaukee in 1996, and now here I was again, landing in a city where fans preferred someone else. The only way to respond was to work as hard as usual. If not harder.

I won them over the first time. There was no guarantee I would win them over again.

10

SOARING IN SEATTLE

Once I recovered from the initial shock, I looked forward to starting over in a different part of the country. Moving around, as you know, was nothing new for me. What was new was the role of leader I was expected to take on. It was my time.

That hadn't been the case in Milwaukee.

Think about it: What veterans would take any advice from some punk in his early twenties? What could he possibly know that they didn't? So, for the most part, I kept my mouth shut. Besides, Sam Cassell did enough talking for the rest of us.

It was more than my youth, to be honest, that had prevented me from seizing a more prominent role. Even when I was the best player on the team, in high school or college, I wasn't very vocal.

Nor did it change much after I was in *He Got Game*. The guard I took down to be Jesus Shuttlesworth, except with close friends and family, went back up when I became Ray Allen again. I would try to set an example, on the court and in the locker room, but I wouldn't hover over guys, trying to get them to do their jobs.

When I arrived in Seattle, no one had to tell me what to do. I could see for myself the team needed a leader now that Gary was gone. You've traded away an obvious Hall of Famer. You better get a leader in return.

Understandably, though, the players seemed a little nervous about the type of leader I might be. Knowing what Gary was like—he and I had our disagreements at the 2000 Olympics—I had a clear sense of where they were coming from. Would I be as demanding? And is that how every franchise player acts?

It sure is. If winning is your ultimate goal.

Gary, in fact, was one of the toughest competitors I faced. During my 18 years in the NBA, I can't think of anyone who played a more in-your-face defense than he did, and he was a gamer on the offensive end, too. You could count on him for about 20 points and 10 assists a night. He played with a great deal of intensity, night after night, and was never afraid to take risks, which is probably why he and George got along so well.

I found out more about Gary by watching the tape of a game from earlier in the season. A player on the team the Sonics were facing made a nifty move to get open, and suddenly here comes Gary, running from the other side of the court to double the guy, and I mean *running*. I couldn't recall seeing a player make a switch like that.

"What kind of defense do you guys call this?" I asked one of the players.

"Dude," he said, laughing, "we don't call that anything. He just made stuff up as he went along."

I would never be that daring. I believed in systems, for better or worse, from my by-the-book upbringing. I don't like surprises, especially on defense; your teammates should have a good idea of where you'll be rotating from in any given set. If anything, Gary may have been *too* capable. Other guys were not able to blossom because, between the way he played and the sheer force of his personality, there was little room left.

"In order for us to be successful," I told the team, "it will take everyone to contribute at both ends. I need you to get rebounds, to give us second-chance opportunities, to do the little things to win games."

In adjusting to the new role, there was a voice in my head; it belonged to George Karl.

I know, it sounds like I must have been haunted, but I wasn't. Oddly enough, it was a voice of reason. Despite the problems we had, George taught me more about basketball than I could begin to remember. I wouldn't have been the player I was without him. So, in Seattle, I found a way to bring out the good George and leave the bad one behind.

Like when he got on me for joking with Sam in practice. I felt he was overreacting at the time, but as I gave the issue more thought, I saw his point. If I were to fool around too much, guys might get the wrong impression, and as a leader now, with people watching my every move, even in practice, I didn't want them to think I didn't take my job seriously.

We knew how to have some fun, too.

On our long plane rides—Seattle felt like it was on another planet, not just a different time zone—five of us used to play a card game called Bourré, similar to Spades, the idea being to take the most tricks in each hand. The pot typically started at $100, and it could go awfully high before you knew where your money went. Winning—or losing—thousands of dollars on one flight wasn't uncommon.

Once, years later, when I was with the Celtics, the security police at the Toronto airport were taking out the lotion I'd mistakenly left in my bag when it hit me what else I'd left there: $35,000 in cash! Back then, players—yours truly included—routinely carried a lot of cash during road trips. The police found the cash and, because I hadn't declared it, were about to keep it. I was detained in some office for an hour, maybe longer, while my teammates on the plane were left wondering what happened to me. I hadn't been detained like that since I stole the box of licorice at Edwards. By the way, they allowed me to keep the cash.

From George, I learned how to let the game come to me, not the other way around. There's a big difference. In my first two years, under Coach Ford, if I didn't touch the ball for five or six possessions, I wasn't very patient when it did come. That's usually when you make mistakes.

George set me straight: Never attempt a difficult shot during the first and second quarters. Get other players involved in the offense.

Then, if you need a bucket in the third quarter—and definitely in the fourth—feel free to take control.

The guys in Seattle realized what I was up to, so whenever I drew a double team and got them the ball where they wanted it—everybody prefers a different spot—they were ready to make a play for themselves or for a teammate.

From the start, I encouraged them to be more accountable to one another. That's the coach's job. In no way was I trying to take it away from Nate, who was more than competent. The fact is, as a player, you get tired of listening to the same voice, especially if that person is constantly telling you what you did wrong.

It doesn't matter if the coach is Gregg Popovich or Phil Jackson or Steve Kerr. Every voice gets old. Which is when you, if you are the leader you claim to be, have to step up. The guys need to hear a different voice.

Say, for example, someone isn't working hard enough on his defense.

"You may think you're hurting the coach," you tell him, "but you are really hurting your teammates."

It wasn't long before I saw steady improvement, on and off the court. A perfect example was Jerome James, our talented seven-foot-one center. Too often, Jerome didn't show up at practice or games as early as he could have, but he always had an excuse, some more original than others. Once, he said he had to stop to help an old lady cross the street. I swear this is true.

"If you had come in earlier," I replied, without missing a beat, "you never would have seen the old lady cross the street."

Jerome also used to wear sweat suits on his way to the locker room before games. Hoping not to sound overbearing, I gave him a little advice.

"How do you think people feel when they see you come dressed like that?" I asked. "Do they think you're ready to play your best? If you show people you're serious about your job, it will change how they view you and it will change how you play."

To his credit, he learned from his mistakes, and so did another player, Rashard Lewis. Though in his fifth season when I joined the Sonics, he was still only 23 and hadn't come close to reaching his potential. I knew he would get there because Rashard possessed something you can't teach: desire. I saw my share of players who could have been marked with the "P" for potential that Coach Dickenman from Connecticut once put next to my name, but who didn't have the desire and never were what they should have been.

"I want to make the money you make," Rashard once said to me.

Good for you, I told him. I've always believed, if you have a goal, don't keep it in your head. Put it out to the universe.

Write it on a wall or in your phone or in a notebook, somewhere you can look at it, so it's no longer a secret you're protecting, maybe from others but mostly from yourself. You protect it out of fear, thinking if you don't achieve your goal, you will never have to admit to yourself, or to anyone else, that you failed.

Some say it isn't wise to put it out to the universe, that it only puts the pressure on yourself. I say: precisely!

There's nothing wrong, by the way, with having the goal of earning as much money as possible. Athletes, remember, have a small window for success that closes fast. Which is why I empathized with Latrell Sprewell, the controversial

All-Star guard from the 1990s and 2000s who was cruci-
fied for saying he had a "family to feed" to explain why he
was rejecting a contract extension that would, in fact, have
resulted in a pay cut.

Get as much as you can; that's always been my attitude.
For anybody who thinks that sounds greedy, I've got news
for you: the owners signing the paychecks make more than
the players. A lot more.

Rashard came in every day to get his shots up, and within
no time, he developed into one of the better young players
in the league. Put him in the post, you knew he'd get the
shot he wanted, and he could hit the three. The payday he
craved would come soon enough.

The entire team started to work just as hard. I loved
to see the guys grow, day by day, and I came up with a
bunch of shooting games after practice to get us even more
prepared to compete. Those shooting games were intense.
Coach Calhoun would have been impressed.

In one game, Around the World, everybody lined up in
the corner and had to hit five straight shots before advancing to the next spot, the elbow three. Whoever made it
through the final spot at the opposite corner first would be
declared the best shooter that day and, better yet, be the
only one who would not have to do any running afterward.

Pity the player who finished last. He had to do suicides,
like we did at UConn, running back and forth between the
baselines. Finish second to last, and you would have to run
from half-court to the backcourt and back to half-court. The
pressure you put on yourself to reach the next spot was akin
to being in a game, which was the point. You would become

so familiar with needing to make a shot to stay alive that you wouldn't panic in a similar situation when the games were for real.

What mattered more than anything was the trust we came to have in one another, and it resulted from those long road trips. There are only so many card games you can play. We talked for hours and hours about life.

The guys asked for my opinion, and I gave it, and if I didn't know something, I said I would get back to them. I became the unofficial liaison between the players and Nate, a role I was happy to assume.

Once, after a win in Minnesota, they asked me to reach out to Nate about getting a rare day off. We definitely needed it. Lots of times, we didn't arrive home until four or five in the morning, and yet we still had to show up for practice at 12:30. Even so, it would require all my powers of persuasion to convince Nate to agree. That's not how he is wired. When he played for the Sonics, in the '80s and '90s, guys routinely went through two-a-days.

"They don't need a day off," he told me. "They're 22 years old."

To set the practice schedule was his right. He was the coach, and I was a player. A player who should have kept his mouth shut.

"It almost seems like Nate forgot what it was like to be a player," I said to my teammates jokingly, though a reporter was nearby, so that wasn't how it came out in the paper.

Nate brought a copy to practice the next day.

"You're killing me for this?" he said.

I apologized right away. I felt awful.

Call it another wake-up call—I'd require quite a few, it

would appear—to remind myself how careful I had to be whenever there was a writer hanging around. Being the face of the franchise, I would make news with almost anything I said.

Look, I don't begrudge these guys for trying to get a scoop. Only they'd have to get a scoop without any help from me.

At 22-30, the Sonics were going nowhere when I came aboard, trailing the better teams (Dallas, San Antonio, Sacramento, Portland, Minnesota, Utah) in the West by a sizable margin. But after my debut, a 106–101 loss to the Lakers, we won five straight. The playoffs weren't out of the question.

Except we couldn't win more than three games in a row the rest of the way, ending up 40-42, four games behind the Phoenix Suns, the number 8 seed. No matter. The future was promising. Besides Rashard and Jerome, Vladimir Radmanovic, a forward from Serbia, was also showing a lot of potential. Vlad had an amazing arc on his jump shots.

If only I had felt better about what was taking place away from the court. There was the issue of food in our locker room, which was not provided unless we asked for it. By contrast, the Mavericks' Mark Cuban not only made sure his team's locker room was well stocked, he also took care of the visiting team. Now that's the kind of owner you want to play for.

Another point of contention was the luggage. Every team gave each player two pieces, complete with the team's logo and their name. Every team, that is, except ours. The owners felt we could pay for our own luggage. They got us the bags eventually, but they wouldn't put our names or numbers on them, saying they would be stolen on the curb. Nonsense. I never heard of any team having its bags ripped off.

All this complaining about food and luggage might seem trivial, but it's not. Our job was to play the game to the best of our abilities, so anything the organization took care of meant there was one less detail we had to be concerned with.

I'm not suggesting these issues kept players from giving a total effort, but I will say this: I have never seen a guy who was treated well by an organization *not* show his appreciation in a way that benefits the team. Players around the league share information with one another, as owners do. We know which teams watch over their players and which don't.

At first, I kept quiet, as I did in Milwaukee, but as a leader, I couldn't avoid speaking up forever.

In the spring of 2004, a reporter asked me how the Sonics conducted business compared to the Bucks. I said the Sonics could do a better job, especially if it hoped to entice the top free agents. I don't recall the article word by word, but I'll never forget the headline in the Seattle paper: "ALLEN WANTS BETTER AMENITIES."

I came across like a spoiled diva instead of somebody addressing real concerns. Even Howard took exception. He called to say that I was being "disingenuous" and offered to give me a tutorial on what it took to run an NBA franchise.

No thank you. I did not need a tutorial to know you can't run a team the way you run Starbucks. This isn't the corporate world. Most owners do not make any real money until they sell the team. In the meantime, you spend what it takes to upgrade the roster and coaching staff—and yes, to provide food in the locker room and luggage for road trips. I said what I had to say and didn't regret it for a second.

That would not be the situation, unfortunately, six months later when it came to comments I made about Kobe Bryant. I'd regret those comments for some time. So much for those earlier wake-up calls.

I was in the locker room in Portland before an exhibition game against the Blazers when the press asked me about our opponent the night before, the Lakers, who had traded Shaq to the Heat in the off-season. I said that I couldn't figure out why Kobe got rid of him, and that every other shooting guard in the league would give anything to play with a center that dominant.

That wasn't all. I said that, in a year or two, Kobe was going to regret the deal and ask for ownership to acquire more players, or to be traded himself, because his team wouldn't be any good.

What I said doesn't seem that horrible, really, but as I wasn't a member of the Lakers or privy to what took place behind the scenes, it was not my business to weigh in on his situation. My attention should have been only on the team I played for. I certainly would have been upset if a player from another organization got involved in our affairs.

Shortly afterward, someone I knew called me out of the locker room before a preseason game against the Lakers in San Diego.

"I just want to give you the heads-up," the guy warned, "because this dude [Kobe] told the big man to give you a hard foul in the game tonight. I want to tell you because you're my man. Be careful out there."

Was I shocked? Not in the least. Nor was I angry, although I did feel it was a little cowardly of him. He could have spoken directly to me instead of sending somebody to do his dirty work; we might have gotten past it. I didn't play that night, by the way, because of a sore ankle. The media tried to keep the controversy going as long as possible, though it died down eventually, replaced by another, no doubt.

In any case, I vowed I would not make the same mistake again, and I didn't.

Three years later, I was in LA, of all places, playing in a golf tournament, when the story broke that Kobe was asking for a trade, as I predicted. Each time I walked near the clubhouse, a reporter approached for a comment. I declined.

Then, in 2011, during the All-Star Game weekend in Los Angeles, I apologized to Kobe. I could tell he appreciated the sentiment.

In the fall of 2004, we couldn't wait to make up for the season before, when we finished 37-45 and did not come close to making the playoffs. It didn't help I missed the first 25 games after injuring an ankle in the preseason.

This year will be different, we told ourselves.

In addition to Rashard, Vlad, Jerome, and me, we had more than capable veterans such as Antonio Daniels, Vitaly Potapenko, and Danny Fortson. Meanwhile, we were counting on Luke Ridnour, a second-year point guard from Oregon, and Nick Collison, a rookie forward from Kansas, to step up.

So what happened on opening night in LA? We lost by 30 . . . to the Clippers! Someone by the name of Bobby Simmons made 13 of his 15 shots. Fortunately, it wasn't a sign of things to come. In fact, we went in the opposite direction, taking our next nine, and 17 of 19.

We were playing at a fast tempo, taking the first good

shot available, similar to the Milwaukee teams I'd been on. Even so, because we weren't on TV much, people in the rest of the country did not take us seriously. That began to change in December after we beat the mighty Spurs on the road. There was no place more difficult to win than in San Antonio. The Sonics are for real, a top national columnist wrote. We were indeed.

Going into the last three and a half weeks of the season, our record was 48-20. Yet I didn't get too carried away. You have to keep the focus always on getting better. Besides, there were more concerns off the court. Prior to the season, with most of the players in the final year of their contract, ownership said they would take care of us if we did our job, but there was reason to believe they didn't mean it.

Case in point: Damien Wilkins.

Damien, the nephew of NBA Hall of Famer Dominique Wilkins, was a rookie guard for us in 2004. He wasn't drafted, but he worked his butt off in training camp to make the roster and was a key part of our success. Which was why we were taken aback when he told us he heard from his agent the organization was thinking about cutting him.

"It doesn't make any sense," I told him. "I'll go talk to management."

Our GM, Rick Sund, agreed. Damien wasn't going anywhere.

Clearly, the agent had gotten his information from someone close to the ownership group. Rick, on this occasion at least, got his way.

Nonetheless, the others remained on edge about where they would wind up after the season ended. So, as a leader, I felt it was time again to speak up.

"Guys," I assured them, "let's take care of business, and we'll get our just dues. And if they don't want to pay us, someone else will."

The message got through: everybody put any anxieties aside, and that was because we had faith in one another. It helped that, as a free agent myself after the season, I would be in the same position as many of them. Yet we won only four of our final 14 to end up 52-30. That's not exactly the kind of momentum you look for heading into the playoffs.

Fortunately, we regrouped to knock off the Sacramento Kings in five games in the first round to set up a battle with the Spurs, who were gunning for their third title in seven years. Forget about Tim Duncan and Tony Parker and Manu Ginobili, as gifted as they were. My mind was on Bruce Bowen. No one guarded me like Bowen did, and I don't mean that as a compliment.

He kicked me when I was on the floor, walked underneath me when I shot the ball, and elbowed me in the stomach. He did everything but tackle me in front of the Alamo. A teammate of mine could drive down the lane uncontested, and Bowen would not move an inch to try to stop him. In the game he was in, there were only two men on the floor, him and me, and his job was to stay glued to my hip. I was being tested, as I was on the playground in South Carolina, and if I allowed Bowen and his bush league tactics to get to me, we wouldn't stand a chance.

What concerned me even more than Bruce Bowen was the fear I saw in a few of my younger teammates, fear that they didn't belong on the same stage with a group as used to winning as the Spurs.

"The pressure is on them," I told the guys. "Everyone expects them to win. No one expects us to."

Sure enough, the Spurs won the first two games in San Antonio, by 22 and 17 points. They played at their usual high level, although we made it much easier for them with 29 turnovers. You can't give it up like that, in the playoffs especially, where each possession is critical.

In Game 3, with the crowd on our side, we regained our composure—we had only 10 turnovers—and escaped with a 92–91 win when Duncan missed a four-footer just before the horn. Phew.

Speaking of misses, I was six for 23 in that game, and that was on me as much as any tactic Bowen resorted to. Jerome and Antonio came through, thank goodness, Jerome hitting all seven of his shots, while Antonio scored 18 points and had eight rebounds. Our defense was outstanding, holding the Spurs without a field goal in the final four minutes and 27 seconds. See, guys, I told you. We belong on the same stage with them.

In Game 4, it was Luke Ridnour's turn.

Luke scored 20 points, 15 during the third quarter, and added six assists and three steals to lead us to a 101–89 victory despite missing Rashard, who had a sprained toe on his left foot. Damien chipped in with 15, while Antonio had 19 points and seven assists. The series, heading back to San Antonio, was tied at two games apiece.

In Game 5, with Rashard still out, along with Vlad, we hung with the Spurs—for a half, the score 50–50. But without those two, we were forced to dig deeper into our bench, and that was probably too much to ask from guys with little experience under this kind of pressure, especially on the road.

San Antonio went on a 17–3 run to start the third quarter, Ginobili hitting a couple of threes, while Bowen stuck to me tighter than ever. I didn't make a shot the entire quarter and missed three free throws after hitting 55 of 59 so far in these playoffs.

Still, our team had grown up quite a bit over the past week. Let's go home, we told ourselves, hold serve, and come back here to give them a battle in Game 7. Maybe the Spurs would feel the anxiety this time.

We'll never know.

In Seattle, we lost by two when Duncan, on a pass from Ginobili, hit a layup with less than a second left. I was able to get off a jump shot from the corner, but with Duncan all over me, I could barely see the basket. The ball hit the rim but didn't come close to going in.

Game over.

Season over.

Everything over.

That's how I felt sitting in front of my locker, like it was the final day of summer camp and everyone was going their separate ways. Which hurt more than the loss itself. There is always another game . . . until, of course, you hang it up for good. But the bond you form with the men by your side is what you value most. Then, and forever.

Jerome was the first to go, signed in July by the Knicks. Good for him. He'd worked hard to rid himself of some poor habits and deserved every penny.

Antonio was next, going to the Wizards. Just like that, two of our core were gone, and you can't afford to lose any of your core if you hope to compete for a championship. You can tinker with it, adding a piece here, a piece there, to build around the other guys, but you can't lose it.

In addition to Jerome and Antonio, we lost somebody else important that summer. We lost Nate McMillan. Paul Allen, the owner of the Portland Trail Blazers, made Nate an offer he couldn't turn down. Nate and I weren't tight— I'm not sure he was close to any player, really—but he had done a very good job.

As for my own future, I chose to stay put, agreeing to a five-year extension for $80 million, with another $5 million in incentives.

Other teams showed interest, the Hawks and the Clippers being the most persistent, but Shannon and I, along with our first child, Rayray, had found a home in Seattle. We loved the city and the people and could think of no better place to raise our family. This franchise had enjoyed some memorable moments—a title in the 1970s, a trip to the Finals in the 1990s—and I won the fans over, just as I did in Milwaukee. I could easily imagine spending the rest of my career there.

Rick Sund thought five years was too many to offer someone at my ripe old age of 30. He presented me with a chart of statistics to prove the average player, once he turns 33 or 34, isn't nearly as productive. Maybe, but I wasn't the average player.

"I truly appreciate and respect where you are coming from," I told Rick. "But you know my habits. You know I'm not a drinker and I don't stay out late. So you should know I'm going to be around a lot longer than a lot of those other guys you mention."

He never showed me any statistics again, and I got the fifth year.

Turning 30, as I did that same month, is usually a time to take stock of one's career, and I was no exception.

One year I went through the entire roster of the team that won the title. I must admit I was jealous. *You kidding me, that guy got a ring too?* But the more I thought about it, the more I realized it would be no shame if I never earned one. It doesn't take anything away from the greatness of Karl Malone or Charles Barkley or John Stockton or Patrick Ewing or other Hall of Famers who didn't win a championship.

Besides, there was still time.

11

SHIPPING UP TO BOSTON

Bob Weiss, one of our assistant coaches, took over for Nate. His calm approach was good for our younger players.

The last thing you ever want is your coaches to always be yelling at you. Believe me, when you screw up, you're the first to know. That's why I stopped looking over at the bench after I threw a bad pass or my man scored a bucket. Coach, if you're not helping me, you're hurting me.

As the 2005–06 season wore on, however, and our mistakes piled up, Bob was too calm. Whenever we lost a game, he would say softly, "That's okay, guys, we'll figure it out tomorrow."

That's fine every so often, but most times we needed a

kick in the ass. Only that wasn't Bob's personality. That was George's, which is why you search for a coach who can be soothing and severe. Doc Rivers was like that. So was Jim Calhoun.

Meanwhile, ownership wasn't willing to wait for tomorrow.

In early January, after just 30 games—we were 13-17—they let Bob go. And I thought Chris, who was fired after two seasons, hadn't been given enough time, though I got the feeling Bob was ready to go, that he believed he'd done everything he could.

Either way, I blamed myself. Whenever a coach is fired, it's on the players. If we do our job, he keeps his. As with Chris, I never got a chance to say good-bye to Bob. That's the way it goes in the NBA: they fire you, and you are out of town before sunset.

The team was in Chicago when Bob Hill, an assistant coach, replaced Weiss and addressed us for the first time. Dressed us down was more like it, *motherfucker this, motherfucker that*. You'd think we had gone 0 for 30 by how disgusted Bob was. "We have a shootaround tomorrow," he said, "and it is going to be one of the hardest shootarounds you've ever had."

I felt as if I were back in freshman year at UConn, going through drill after drill. We never practiced that hard during a shootaround under Coach Weiss, or Nate for that matter. Mind you, I'm not complaining. We needed the work.

Bob was tough on me on occasion, but he didn't yell like Chris did. He would often go out of his way to praise me. I would be driving home after a game, and Bob would give me a call.

"Listen, man, I just want to let you know how awesome you were tonight," he'd say.

That meant a lot to me. I can't think of another coach I played for who showed that much respect.

Too bad we didn't reward his efforts with more victories. In the end, it still comes down to talent in this league, and we did not have enough—or to put it more kindly, the talent we did have was raw. Our two young bigs, Johan Petro from France and Robert Swift from Bakersfield, California, who we drafted out of high school in 2004, needed a veteran such as Jerome James to help them develop—the same Jerome James who was then with the Knicks.

The losses mounted, and we finished 35-47, the worst record for a team I was on since my rookie season in Milwaukee. The series against the Spurs seemed like a lifetime ago.

I would be lying if I said that losing didn't bother me, but it didn't bother me as much as you might imagine. I enjoyed the guys I was playing with immensely and felt strongly that, if we continued to dedicate ourselves, we could get back to where we were in 2005. Young and impressionable, they didn't have too high of an opinion of themselves, and that would be to their benefit.

Bob used to tell me all the time: "I don't know how you do it. You come out and play hard every single night, and do your best despite us not having a real chance to win."

Honestly, I never thought of it like that. Winning is not just about scoring more points than the other team; it's also about giving the game everything you have, regardless of who you play against or how talented your teammates may be. I learned long ago to focus on what you can control, not on what you can't.

Out of my control, for example, was the future of the franchise in Seattle.

In July 2006, Howard sold the Sonics to a group from Oklahoma City, where the team, renamed the Thunder, would play starting in 2008. I'd always believed the Sonics would never leave Seattle, given such enthusiastic support from the fans at KeyArena. Turns out, those fans represented a relatively small sample size; perhaps the organization hadn't done nearly enough to establish a bond throughout the community.

Also out of my control was the condition of my ankles, even though there was no one to blame but myself. Instead of worrying about what George said about me to the press, I should have sat out a few games, perhaps more, back in 2001 or 2002. Since I hadn't, the scar tissue in my ankles had built up, and the pain had grown almost unbearable. In April 2007, with the team once again headed for the NBA lottery, I underwent surgery to remove bone spurs in both ankles, missing the final 16 games.

While I recovered, I looked forward to the upcoming season, especially after I had lunch downtown in June with our new general manager, Sam Presti.

Sam wanted to know everything about the team, and I was glad to fill him in, as I'd done with Senator Kohl. I was confident that Sam would make the right moves, starting with the upcoming draft. The ping-pong balls bouncing in our favor, for a change, we would have the number 2 pick, which meant, barring a late surprise, we would choose Kevin Durant, a can't-miss forward from the University of Texas. Things finally were looking up.

I was at home with Shannon, Tierra, Rayray, and the most recent addition to the family, Walker, born the year before, when Commissioner Stern made it official: Durant it was. Hallelujah! With KD, Rashard, and myself, we would have an offense capable of competing in the run-and-gun Western Conference.

There was only one problem: it was no longer *we;* it was *they.*

On the same night—what was it with me and draft nights?—the Sonics traded me to Boston for Delonte West, Wally Szczerbiak, and the rights to the Celtics' number 5 pick, Jeff Green, a forward from Georgetown. Just like that, I was on the move again.

So what? If anything, I should have been overjoyed, right? After all, this was not some run-of-the mill franchise they were sending me to. This was the Boston Celtics, as close as it comes to royalty in the NBA. Plus, I would be only an hour from family and friends in Connecticut.

Why, then, did I have such mixed feelings?

Well, for one thing, I was upset with how the trade went down. Once again, I got the news from the media instead of the team.

I also felt that Sam had led me to believe at our lunch that I was an important part of his plans for the future.

What a performance. He should have been in Hollywood, not Seattle. If only he had told me, "Ray, we have this deal on the table. I don't know if it's going to happen, but I just wanted you to know about it so you can be prepared." I would have thanked him for the respect he was showing me and wished him luck. I wasn't some rookie. I knew basketball was a business.

Besides, whenever you're traded, there's more to consider than what team you'll be playing for. Shannon and I had a circle of friends we'd have to leave behind. I felt like I did when I was growing up. The difference now was that I was the one getting new orders, not my father.

Leaving Seattle felt the same as leaving Milwaukee. I didn't do what I'd set out to do, and that was to win a championship. In both cases, decisions were made that didn't bring us closer to reaching that goal, and the window to win—so narrow to begin with in this league—had closed. For good.

Yet, once again, the disappointment didn't last long. We were soon on a plane to Boston.

To a city, and a time, my family and I would cherish forever.

Walking into the Boston Garden and seeing the numbers worn by Bird, McHale, Parish, Havlicek, Russell, Cousy, and other heroes from the past made it sink in: I'm really a Celtic!

I thought it might happen before, on draft night in 1996, when I got the call from Red Auerbach, but it wasn't meant to be. Not yet.

From the start, Danny Ainge, the Celtics' GM, could not have made me feel more welcome. Danny explained that acquiring me was just the first move. He was constantly looking for ways to improve the team, calling me to ask my opinion of one person or another. I can't think of any other general manager who would seek that much input from a player when he was trying to put his team together.

Danny's next move was to bring in someone I knew very well—someone who, like me, was looking for that first ring and starting to run out of time. This player and I met when we were kids in South Carolina, sharing a ride to Columbia and eager to find out how we might stack up against the best players in the state, talking about Michael Jordan, the girls we knew, and the other things boys with big dreams back then liked to talk about.

Yup, Kevin Garnett.

All these years later, Kevin and I still had a great amount of respect for each other, although we didn't cross paths too often. I got the feeling that because he came in a year before I did—he was drafted out of high school by Minnesota—it was important for him to make it clear to me that he was the veteran and I was the newcomer. He used to tell people I made him run errands when we were kids, such as picking up Gatorade at the corner store. Which wasn't true.

"We couldn't afford to buy Gatorades in those days," I told Kevin.

Shortly after I joined the Celtics, he called me. The trade talks between Boston and Minnesota were heating up, and Kevin had some genuine concerns. Playing in Boston wouldn't be the same as playing in Minnesota. He'd yearned to be on a bigger stage, and now would have to come through.

"Man, I don't know how this is going to work," he said. "I got to really step up my game."

There was absolutely nothing wrong with Kevin's game—during the 2006–07 season, he averaged 22.4 points and a league-high 12.8 rebounds—but NBA players are not robots. We too have doubts from time to time.

"You just do what you do, and everything will be fine," I assured him.

Soon it became official: Kevin was coming to Boston,

thanks to a deal Danny swung with his ex–Celtics teammate from the 1980s, Kevin McHale, the vice president of the Timberwolves.

With Kevin and Paul Pierce, the Celtics' longtime star, I was now part of a new Big Three, more potent than the Big Three in Milwaukee. The fans were excited and sensed an opportunity for their team's 17th banner, the first in more than 20 years. Far be it from me to lower anyone's expectations, but I wasn't ready to book the parade down Boylston Street just yet. I knew from experience that too much can go wrong, and fast.

Perhaps there is no better example than the 2003–04 Los Angeles Lakers. That season, to a team that already had Shaq and Kobe, they added future Hall of Famers Karl Malone and Gary Payton. Seriously, how could a team so gifted *not* win a championship? That's easy. In the Finals, they came up against a very formidable Detroit squad coached by Larry Brown. The result: Pistons in five.

Kevin, you see, was on to something—how *was* this going to work?—and it had to do with how he, Paul, and I would fit into our new roles. Three egos, one ball. Do the math.

There was only one solution.

"This is Paul's team," Kevin and I told our coach, Doc Rivers, right away. "We're here to help the team out however best we can. He's the captain, and we're not trying to step on his toes."

As for the relationship between Kevin and I, that was another matter entirely. We were not teenagers anymore; we were men, with much different habits and personalities. As we found out in Rome, where the team went in early October to play a few preseason games. My doctor suggested

I hold off for a little longer, as I was still recovering from ankle surgery, but I couldn't wait to work out with my new teammates and see how I fit in.

Not very well. Not with Kevin.

It started innocently enough, me dribbling the basketball in front of my locker before we went on the court for our first game. I'd been dribbling before games for as long as I could remember. Not once did anybody voice an objection. Until then.

"How long are you going to be doing that?" Kevin asked.

"Doing what?" I responded.

"Dribbling the basketball. Are you going to be doing that the whole time?"

"Yes, this is what I do to get ready. We're about to play a basketball game."

Neither of us was willing to give an inch. That's what happens when you have two alpha dogs in the same room, each determined to impose his will on the other. As franchise players, we were used to having our way.

"No, you're not going to do that," he said.

"You can't tell me what to do," I told him. "You do what you do, and I do what I do."

Gee, can two grown men be any more juvenile? The rest of the guys, meanwhile, did not say a word, although no doubt they were thinking to themselves: *This isn't good.* They were curious to see which alpha dog would be the first to back down.

Me, as it turned out. I realized you have to give in every so often for the good of the team, although I now had a feeling this season was going to challenge us all.

From then on, I stuck to my routine as much as possible

while trying to respect how others prepared for games. In the few minutes before a game started, I had to really watch myself. I would be in the huddle, getting instructions from Doc, and as soon as we put our hands in to say, "Celtics on three," Kevin would thrust his arm into the air and give me a bump if I was too close, or anyone else was. The message was impossible to miss:

Get out of my way! This is my space!

And God forbid you're on the opposing team and say something that gets under his skin.

Like what happened one night in the 2007–08 season against the Bulls. After Kevin hit one of his trademark step-back jumpers, Joakim Noah, their rookie center, told him, "Hey, big fella, that was a nice move. You've got to teach me that."

There was nothing wrong with what Noah said. Players, especially those new to the league, always hope to pick up tips they can adopt for their own games. Noah looked up to Kevin. Only Kevin was not about to teach him a damn thing—except to know better than to ever speak to him again.

"Get off my dick," he told Noah.

I couldn't help but laugh. That was KG for you. If you're on his team, he will die for you. If you're not, he won't give you the time of day.

Which is why, of the dozens of teammates I ever had, in college or the NBA, if I had to choose only one to play with, it would be Kevin Garnett. No one else comes close.

Not because he lit up the stat sheet with points, rebounds, blocks, assists, steals, you name it, and not because he could play three or four positions. But because he never took a game off. A *possession* off. I can't say that of anyone else I played with, and I played with some of the best.

Me as a little guy, three years old.

Me, Mom, Kim, Dad, John, Kristie, and Talisha in the first official family portrait we ever took while stationed overseas in England.

Dad and Mom, Germany, 1977.

(above) Edwards AFB, me at ten years old on the first organized basketball team I ever played on—disregard my ashy knees.

(left) This is a photo of my mom doing her thing in her semi-pro days with the Bentwaters Lady Phantoms. Flo, aka "Truck," is seen running toward the action (not dribbling the ball).

(left) Hillcrest Wildcats circa 1991–1992 season; my junior year in high school.

(above) My dad and his hoop team the Edwards Rattlers at Edwards AFB in California, sitting in front of a B-1 Bomber on the flight line.

(right) Dad, Mom, and me. This was taken while I was home on summer break from UConn—it was a shot for *Sports Illustrated* on Shaw AFB posing with the F-16s.

(below) Tierra and me doing a little karaoke at home.

(right) This was a picture taken of Shannon and me after she surprised me with a party on my twenty-fourth birthday—we were babies.

(left) Me and our boys in our home in Miami (2013) for our Christmas card shoot. Rayray, me, Walker, Wystan, and Wynn.

(below) Me and the fam getting geared up for the Championship Parade in 2013.

(left) Rayray and me cruising the beach in Hawaii.

(right) This was taken while I was watching a UConn football game during my official visit to Connecticut in 1993.

(below) Me trying to stay in front of the greatest player to ever play the game.

(above) The Big Three—us versus everybody else.

(below) Doc Rivers and me during one of our many sideline meetings, in which he would frequently tell me to keep everybody calm out there in tough situations.

(above) EPIC. Making this shot was the moment that every kid dreams of!

(left) There's nothing like hitting a game-winning shot at home to bring the crowd to their feet.

(below) The King and I.

Though I have to tell you, I was just as intense as he was. The only difference was, I didn't go out of my way to show it, and why should I have to? You don't have to bump someone, or scream, or have a permanent scowl on your face to prove how intense you are. You prove it by being dedicated to your craft, night in and night out. So what if others don't see that intensity? You know it's there, and that's what matters.

Looking back, given the problems that would later surface between us, there are things KG and I should have said to each other from the start, and it wasn't as if we didn't have our chances.

One night, before the trip to Rome, we met for dinner at a steakhouse in Boston. We talked about how much it hurt to be on losing teams for a large part of our careers and how much we wanted to earn a ring. What I wish we had talked about was something deeper, more personal. That he and I would support each other no matter what issues were to come between us.

Let's never forget we're brothers and that we go back a long way, I would have told him.

Instead, on the very same night, KG found something else to compete with me over.

"I'll take the check," I told the waitress.

"No," he said, "I tip way better than him, so you better give me the check."

There was no point in arguing with the guy. What struck me was that he felt the need to be seen as being superior to me, even in something as petty as this. The two of us had never been out to dinner. So how did he know what kind of tipper I was?

Perhaps if we'd said the things I wish we said, we could have had a good laugh—*look, we're competing already!*—and decided to split the bill. Then, when we had bigger conflicts later on, such as the dribbling incident, perhaps we could have resolved them as well.

One thing we had in common, however, was our willingness to sacrifice. For me, that meant I'd no longer be counted on to score at least 20 points a game, as I did in every season from 1999 through 2007. No problem. What exactly did those points get me, anyway? Not a trip to the Finals, I'll tell you that.

Still, not being the number-one option would take some getting used to. In Seattle, I averaged roughly 19 shots per game. By comparison, during my first five starts with Boston, I averaged about 13. So, instead of taking almost any shot to work myself into a good shooting rhythm, I had to be more selective, waiting for the best first shot that was available; my goal, you see, was always to shoot at least 50 percent. That's how efficient Michael Jordan was. People say Michael took a lot of shots, and he did, but he averaged almost 50 percent over his whole career—49.7 percent, to be exact.

If anything, I might have been too unselfish. It wasn't that way at first. Any time I had a decent look at a three, I let it go. Except Doc would then get in my face during the next time-out.

"You see Kevin Garnett in the block," he said, "you throw him the ball."

Nothing against KG—he was almost automatic in the lane—but to that point in my career, in similar situations, the coaches had always urged me to take the shot. Which I did, and it made no difference who was in the block. Some years, I hit over 40 percent of my threes. Besides, if I had thrown the ball to KG he would have given it right back and come out to set a screen for me. There were times we had to tell him to shoot more.

As the season wore on and he saw how hard I worked to prepare myself for each game, Doc became more comfortable with me taking the shot and actually encouraged it. The three became a weapon for us.

"You guys have the best shooter in the NBA on your team," Doc told the others. "Get him the ball. I never mind if Ray Allen takes the shot."

Yet I still didn't get enough touches, which frustrated me the most when I was going through a rough stretch. Usually, in those situations, the coach calls a play to get the guy a good look. See the ball fall through the net just once, and it's amazing how quickly your confidence will return. Doc called plays constantly for Paul Pierce.

"We got to get Paul going," he'd tell us.

I wish, every once in a while, he would have said, "We got to get Ray going." I was someone, after all, they counted on to hit a three or make the free throws to put the other team away.

"Mariano, we need you," my teammates would say, referring to the New York Yankees' star closer Mariano Rivera. "Go in there and make a shot."

I was ready to do just that, but it would've been much easier if I had been able to warm up, as Rivera did, instead of going through long periods without touching the ball. In Seattle, I rarely missed a free throw during the fourth quarter. Having had the ball in my hands on most of the possessions down the stretch, I stayed in rhythm.

In retrospect, I should have talked to Doc much sooner

about those concerns, just as I waited too long to talk to George. No one is going to speak up for you if you don't speak up for yourself. My hesitation shows how much winning a championship meant to me. I was not going to be blamed for disrupting the harmony we worked hard to build.

Likewise, I was careful in how I dealt with Paul.

Paul and I had less in common than KG and me, especially when it came to how we approached the game. He was focused when he was matched up against LeBron or Kevin Durant or any of the other top players, but not necessarily if the man he was guarding wasn't among the elite.

"I'm taking the night off," he'd tell us.

Paul was obviously joking, but the fact he even said it bothered me. Because you never knew if that mind-set might affect his performance and cost us the game. We were fighting hard for home-court advantage for the whole playoffs, and one game might make the difference.

Once, he tried to get me to think along the same lines.

"Hey, Ray, you got a night off," he said after noticing that the player I would be defending wasn't highly regarded.

"No, I don't," I told him emphatically. He didn't say another word.

No player should ever have a night off. The worst player in the NBA would not be *in* the NBA if he weren't good, which means he has the potential to beat you on any given night. And if you think you have to put forth a greater effort against the top players, you clearly aren't giving enough of an effort against everyone else.

As the year unfolded, I was glad to see the effect KG and I had on Paul. Watching us get our shots up and hit the weight room, day after day, he became more serious in the way he prepared. He no longer joked about taking nights off. Come the fourth quarter, if we needed a hoop, Paul was who Doc relied on most, with good reason. No one delivered in the clutch like him.

Our point guard was Rajon Rondo, and I couldn't have gotten along with him any better. He became like a little brother to me, spending hours at my house asking about contracts and other parts of the business. I was his mentor, a role I was eager to take on. I understood that the more success Rondo had, the more success we'd have as a team.

He wasn't the greatest shooter in the world, but that didn't stop him from having a major impact. Rondo was a special player in how he could spot the open man for an easy basket and slide into the paint to snatch rebounds away from guys three or four inches taller. In his second season, there was no limit to how good this kid could be.

Rondo was confident, that's for sure. Perhaps too confident. In doing some research on him—I found it helpful to learn as much as I could about new teammates—I came upon an interview where he was asked if he was excited to be on the same team with Paul, KG, and myself. Rondo's response was something to the effect of: they are going to have to get used to playing with *me*.

Wow. In hindsight, it was probably something I should've paid more attention to, given how our relationship would fall apart, but at the time I thought it showed the kind of moxie you want to see in a young player, especially the point guard, who sets the tone.

Our center was Kendrick Perkins. Perk wasn't afraid to mix it up with anyone. Let your man get by you, he would be there in the paint to bail you out, as was KG.

Then there was our bench, and I'd stack it up against any bench in the league: we had guys who could score, like Eddie House, and guys who could stop the other team from scoring, like James Posey and Tony Allen. When I watched James guard his man, being a hound in front of the ball, it hit me for the first time how much of a skill playing defense truly is.

For many years, I was so good offensively that none of my coaches took me to task on the other side of the ball. I wish they had. The one major regret of my career is that I wasn't better on the defensive end. I always thought I was putting forth the effort, but I didn't grasp what it took, like where my body position needed to be at all times. I could slide my feet and cut off the angles, but I didn't know what to do with my arms and upper body.

Don't get me wrong; I wasn't a liability on defense. Far from it.

In the 2001 playoffs against Philadelphia, I played Iverson about as tough as you can. Knowing his moves, I stayed in front of him. He got his points, averaging 30 per game, but he shot just 34 percent from the field. He wasn't the only reason we lost the series.

Now, with Doc, I was finally with a coach who made defense the number-one priority, and a guy, KG, who was one of the better defensive players in the league. With them showing the way, in practice after practice, I worked harder than ever at that part of my game, and it paid off.

"We have to be the best defensive team in the NBA," Doc used to tell us. "That's what's going to win us a championship."

And to think that KG and I had felt that Doc was the

one big unknown heading into the season. We knew he was a good person, but we had no idea what kind of coach he'd be. Plenty of former players weren't the best coaches. KG was most concerned with how much running there would be in training camp. We'd been with coaches who ran us ragged. Our bodies were younger then.

Doc put us at ease right away.

"You guys are veterans," he said. "I know the work you put in. There isn't going to be a lot of running."

He was just as understanding once the season began, making sure to conserve our energy. If we played on a Monday and Tuesday and the next game was on Thursday, the team wouldn't practice on Wednesday and there wouldn't be a shootaround on Thursday. He knew what it felt like to run out of energy in the fourth quarter, when most games are won or lost.

Our rest mattered so much that Doc brought in an actual sleep doctor, who put training aids on our heads to monitor if we were getting enough sleep. Unlike other teams I'd been on, I never caught anyone yawning in the gym. A lot of coaches assume that because we're so gifted and athletic, we can do anything. I wish. Our bodies break down like everybody else's. When I got home from practice, I needed a nap.

Doc treated us like men. Take, for instance, our practice schedule. He asked us what time we wanted to practice. He didn't tell us. Other coaches tell you.

They tell you when to be at practice, when to be at the shootaround, when to be on the bus. There is very little they don't tell you, and it's no fun to be treated like that, believe me, especially if you have been in the league for a while. You begin to think you're back in junior high. So, by allowing us to have a greater say, we did not feel like laborers serving ownership; we felt a sense of ownership ourselves, which makes a big difference. If you feel you own a piece of something, you will work harder to make it a success.

Doc also worked on our minds, as the top coaches in every sport do, looking for ways to make us feel as one.

The day before the team took off for Rome, he had KG, Paul, and me meet him at his apartment in Boston at 8:00 AM sharp. Hey, Doc, with all due respect, couldn't this perhaps wait until the next day, or until later in the morning?

Apparently not. The three of us got there at eight, and the next thing we knew, a Duck Boat—one of those boats that can go on land or water—pulled up to where we were standing by Doc's building. These were the boats the Patriots and Red Sox rode on during their championship parades.

Get on board, Doc said. He wasn't kidding. With the whole boat to ourselves, we made our way slowly through the neighborhoods, and then down an embankment and into the water. He didn't wait long to make his point. He rarely did.

"This is what we're going to do at the end of the year," he said, "and it's important that you guys know what it feels like."

I'm not sure what KG and Paul thought about taking this unexpected tour of the city, but I thought it was a wonderful idea.

Basketball is a business—I am not suggesting otherwise—but sometimes you have to be corny and be willing to feel like a kid again. Doc understood the right balance between fun and hard work. If we lost a few games in a row, he would cancel practice and take us to a movie or come up with another activity to get our minds away from the game.

Most coaches I've been around would never dare try something like that. They play by the book, from the first day of training camp to the last game of the season.

A break? You guys don't need a break. You need to work harder. See you at the facility an hour earlier tomorrow, and be ready to do some extra running. I don't care how long we have to stay here—we will turn this thing around!

Such a hard-line approach will not pay off. Remember, we're not robots.

Sitting in the Duck Boat, I felt part of something larger than myself.

Not that I didn't feel part of something larger in Milwaukee and Seattle. The difference was that here, in Boston, with this coach, this group of players, and these fans, I felt it more intensely than ever. We were on a mission to win a championship, led by a coach who helped us see more than what was in front of us at the moment.

Would we get there? It was impossible to know. The bounces might go our way, or they might not. Somebody could get hurt. Somebody could lose focus. There is only so much under your control.

Yet the fact that the organization had the resources to take us on the Duck Boat ride proved it would possess the resources for another trip, to the Finals, to be followed by another boat ride in June.

First things first. Off to Rome we went, where we bonded in ways I don't believe we would have if we had remained at our practice facility in Waltham, outside of Boston. Separated from family and friends, we were forced to extend ourselves to one another. You spend so much time with your teammates you think you know them. You don't. But far from home, with no place you have to be, you learn who they are and what they want.

We spent hours sitting on the famous Spanish Steps, doing little but watch people go by. Curious, as usual, I rented a scooter on the second day and parked it outside the hotel. Every day, after practice, I drove around to see the Rome where people work and live, not just the tourist attractions.

From Rome, we headed to London for another exhibition game. Then it was back to the United States. We'd been gone two weeks, though it felt a lot longer, in a good way; that's how much we had grown as a team.

The 2007–08 season was about to start. For the first time in my career, I was in a place where people expected us to do something special.

I wouldn't have wanted it any other way.

12

RING IN THE NEW YEAR

Opening night in Boston was quite a night. The fans cheered for us louder than any fans I'd been around, and it would be that loud the whole season. Every night, even on nights when it was obvious we didn't have our best stuff, they were loyal to the very end, willing us to wins we probably didn't deserve.

"Is it always like this?" the Rockets' Tracy McGrady once asked me. "I feel like I'm in the playoffs."

The support wasn't just something I felt at games. I felt it when I went for a walk or pumped gas or was out to dinner with my family.

"Hey, we just want to let you know we're rooting for you guys," they'd say. "Let's do it!"

The fans at Boston Garden were so engaged that they would be in their seats at least a half-hour before tip-off. They loved to watch us and the other team go through warm-ups. You almost worried that the game, for their sake, would not start soon enough. Then, once it did start, they saw their job as more than rooting for the good guys. They tried to intimidate the bad guys. *You are not welcome here, and we will see that you don't forget it.*

I can't imagine ever hearing a Celtics fan say, "It doesn't matter if I go to the game or not." Whether they were sitting up high close to the rafters or courtside, they felt that they, not just the players, had to bring their "A" game night after night. Or they would be letting us down.

And, man, did they know their basketball. Nothing got by them.

Run a questionable play near the end of a game and, believe me, you would hear about it, either on the court or when people approached you around town. I was our top free-throw shooter, but every so often, to get Paul in rhythm, we agreed he would go to the line when the other team was called for a technical.

"Why isn't Allen shooting it?" the fans would want to know.

Even how they sounded was different from anything I was familiar with. The noise kept rising, and rising, until everything began to shake and you felt like the whole building might come down.

And to think that Boston, I'd heard for the longest time, was a city where a black athlete might not feel very welcome.

I have been to a lot of cities in America, and racism exists everywhere, whether people want to believe it or not. The whites live in a certain part of town, the blacks in another. Boston, I believe, received its reputation due to the difficult times that Bill Russell and other black players faced in the 1950s and 1960s.

The times haven't changed much. Look what happened in the spring of 2017, when fans at Fenway Park shouted the n-word at Adam Jones, an outfielder for the Baltimore Orioles. The Red Sox have to take whatever steps necessary to make sure incidents like this don't happen again anywhere.

On opening night, we beat the Washington Wizards, 103–83, Paul leading the way with 28 points. KG, meanwhile, was everywhere: 22 points, 20 rebounds, five assists, three blocks, and three steals. I chipped in with 17, including two three-pointers.

You can't base anything on a single performance, but it sure felt as if this show was destined to be a hit. Not that we were there to entertain; we were there to work.

Talking trash was also not our style. Gilbert Arenas, the point guard for the Wizards, had bragged how he, Caron Butler, and Antawn Jamison were the better Big Three. We didn't need to respond, except on the court.

The next game, in a 98–95 victory over the Raptors in Toronto, I scored my first big basket as a Celtic, a three from the corner with 2.6 seconds to go in OT, one of seven threes I hit that night.

For years, prior to KG and I arriving in Boston, the other team at the end of a game would force Paul to beat them.

Now, on any given day, the defense could not be certain who would take the last shot: Paul, KG, or me. And if they tried to double any of us, we'd find the open man.

Which reminds me of a conversation the three of us had with a writer in Boston before the season started.

"I have a question I want you guys to answer, all at the same time," she said. "Who is going to get the ball for the last shot?"

I said, "The open man." Paul said, "Ray." KG said, "One of them."

What struck me was how different the answer would have been the year before, or any year. Each of us would not have hesitated for a second to say, "Me." Each of us would have been right.

We kept going, winning our next six to reach 8-0, before a 104–102 loss on the road to the Orlando Magic. About a week later, we took on the Cavs in Cleveland.

With 23.1 seconds left in regulation and the game tied at 92, I went to the line for two free throws. No problem. The first one went in . . . and out! What? How could I miss in a moment like this?

Missing the first one, though, was not where I messed up. *Thinking* about the first one as I was getting ready to shoot the second was.

Still angry with myself, I didn't focus on my routine, and, as I'm sure you know by now, routine is everything in this sport. In free throws, I'd locate the center nail on the floor with my right foot, mimic my follow-through without the ball, catch the ball from the ref, roll it in my hands, dribble three times, roll it again, and shoot.

Every time. Everywhere. It was my way of distracting myself from any anxiety I might feel.

I missed again.

We ended up losing in overtime, 109–104, LeBron with 38 points and 13 assists. I was upset, as you can imagine, though it hit me there was a real learning opportunity there, and damn if I was going to miss that as well: it does no good to dwell on missing a free throw, or on missing a three-pointer, or on missing a teammate who is wide open. The game moves too rapidly. The mind must move at the same speed or you'll be left behind. Focus instead on the next free throw. The next three-point shot. The next pass.

There was another lesson I learned that night. Who was I to assume that I couldn't miss a free throw? I didn't shoot 100 percent from the line. I shot 90 percent. That means missing one out of every 10, and this just happened to be the one.

Lessons learned, I moved on.

The next day, though, I got a call from my former teammate Sam Cassell, who was playing for the Clippers.

"I wouldn't have missed those free throws RayAllen, RayAllen," he said.

Knowing Sam, his call didn't bother me one bit. He was right: he wouldn't have missed them.

Two days later, we began a new winning streak, beating the Knicks, 104–59, holding them to 30 percent from the field. They didn't score more than 18 in any quarter. We then held the Heat to 85, and the Cavs to 70. In the month of December, we lost only once, by two points to the Pistons at the Garden. By early January, we were 29-3, the identical win-loss total the Bulls had in 1996 when they went on to win a then-record 72 games.

Believe me, though, winning was not nearly as automatic as we made it seem. Every game felt like the Super Bowl, every team eager to pull off the upset, and keeping your edge over an 82-game season is next to impossible.

Thank goodness for Doc. He knew how to motivate us, often with a quote from history that he would write on the wall or stick in our locker. On Martin Luther King Day, we spoke about what Dr. King did for each of us to get to where we were. Doc was the first coach I played for where it was not just about basketball; it was about reaching his players as human beings too.

My favorite quote was from Teddy Roosevelt's 1910 speech, "The Man in the Arena":

It is not the critic who counts; not the man who points out how the strong man stumbles, or where the doer of deeds could have done them better. The credit belongs to the man who is actually in the arena, whose face is marred by dust and sweat and blood; who strives valiantly; who . . . at the best knows in the end the triumph of high achievement, and who, at the worst, if he fails, at least fails while daring greatly, so that his place shall never be with those cold and timid souls who neither know victory nor defeat.

The choice is yours. You can be like Kenny, the kid who said I wouldn't make the team in junior high, or my teammate at Hillcrest who told everyone I'd be an alcoholic.

Or you can be the one who dares greatly, in whatever you do with your life. Any time I hear somebody being too critical of an individual in the public eye, I think: *At least that person is putting his reputation on the line. When have you, the critic, shown that kind of courage?*

A day rarely goes by when I don't share the "The Man in the Arena" with someone; it means that much to me. I was also inspired by a video Doc showed us in the playoffs one year, called "Battle at Kruger." The battle is between a group of lions, a herd of buffalo, and a crocodile. Bottom line: If we go our separate ways, we don't stand a chance. But if we stick together, we can beat anyone.

Earlier, along the same lines, Doc introduced us to Ubuntu, a philosophy practiced by none other than Nelson Mandela.

The point is that, to be the best you can be, everybody around you also has to be the best they can be. Ubuntu became our mantra for the rest of the season. Before going onto the court, we would join together in a circle, raise our arms, and remind ourselves to play for one another, not for any individual glory.

"Ubuntu, be our brothers' keeper," we'd shout.

Doc brought in the leader of a basketball organization from South Africa, who told us that, in his community, people constantly reached out to anyone who was in need.

James Posey, who had been in the league since 1999, also had a way to motivate the guys.

All he had to do was show us something the rest of us did not have—his ring. During practice, Doc put the starters on one side of the court, the subs on the other.

James, being one of the subs, kept making the same comment.

"That's okay, y'all got no rings," he would say. He won that championship with the Heat in 2006.

He was kidding around, but hearing him say it over and over had a real effect on us. We never lost sight of what we were chasing.

Then, in March, we signed Sam Cassell, who had been waived by the Clippers a week before. Sam, at 38, was well past his prime, but he could still shoot and run an offense, which we sorely needed on the second unit. Sam also would help keep us from getting complacent. Looking back, I can think of at least five games we had given away.

Two weeks later, Sam scored 17 points in a victory over the Spurs in San Antonio. We won the next night in Houston, and in Dallas two nights later. That's what you call the "Texas Three-Step." Taking 11 of our final 12, we finished the season at 66-16, securing the number 1 seed in the Eastern Conference and home-court advantage throughout the postseason.

Of course, there was no reason to celebrate yet. Nothing less than a title, and another ride on the Duck Boat, would be acceptable.

Doc made sure we understood what would be required going forward.

"We need to cut out all the extracurricular activities," he told us, "so you can take care of yourselves. If that means you guys need to stop having sex, or need to have more sex, I don't care. Whatever it is, I need you to make the sacrifices to be ready for the playoffs."

I never thought that having more sex was a "sacrifice," but what did I know?

Atlanta was our opponent in the first round. The Hawks had won only 37 games, 29 fewer than we did. Sweeping them was a real possibility, especially after we took the first two at the Garden, by 23 and 19 points. There was no sense in allowing the series to go on a moment longer than it needed to.

Or you can do what we did: lose the next two in Atlanta and make it a series again. Either these were not the Hawks we saw during the season or we weren't who we pretended to be.

Back in Boston for Game 5, we cruised again, 110–85, as I hit five threes.

"Guys," I told my teammates afterward, "we have to go to Atlanta and get this next game."

Game 6, in any playoff series, is huge. Say you're up three games to two and lose. That means it goes down to a Game 7, and strange things can happen in a Game 7. You can even make the argument that the visiting team has an advantage. Everyone expects the home team to win.

In any case, we were about to find out. That's because Game 6 was much like the other two games in Atlanta: the Hawks, with six players scoring in double figures, beat us, 103–100. Who *were* these guys?

Now that a Game 7 was here, I was a bit antsy. Typically, on the night before a game, I don't think much about it; the pressure can drive you insane. Instead, I prefer to keep myself occupied by playing with my kids, watching a little television, reading a book, anything but basketball.

This time I couldn't stop thinking about it. In the middle of the night, I texted my teammates, the message the same to each one:

"Let's go get it tomorrow. We have an opportunity."

Most of them were awake, as I figured they'd be. We'd worked so hard to get to this point that the thought of our dream ending this quickly was almost too much to bear.

You should approach a Game 7 as you would any game. Play hard. Remember where you're supposed to be. Don't try to be a hero when somebody else has a clearer shot. You know, the usual. Except this isn't the usual, and there is no reason to pretend it is. In that case, use that nervous energy to play the game of your life.

Mission accomplished. We jumped out to a sizable lead, were up 18 at the half, and coasted home. KG was tremendous, with 18 points and 11 rebounds, while Perk had 10 boards and five blocks. The final: 99–65.

Our next opponent was the Cleveland Cavaliers, who won the East the year before, when LeBron was just 22. I was looking forward to it, having averaged around 24 per game against them during the regular season.

So you won't believe what happened in Game 1 at the Garden. I did not score a single point. In 37 minutes, I attempted only four shots and didn't get to the line. Last time I was shut out was . . . man, I can't remember. Each time I came off a pick, there were two guys on me. We wound up getting the win, 76–72, but a work of art it was not. Thank goodness LeBron was off, going 2 for 18 and committing 10 turnovers.

Two days later, we prevailed again to take a 2–0 lead, holding the Cavs once more to less than 40 percent from the field. Except, like the Atlanta series, we couldn't get it done on the road, losing Game 3 by 24 and Game 4 by 11. In the four games we had yet to break 90. That happened just 11 times the whole *season*.

The reporters went looking for answers. The reporters in Boston were always looking for answers.

Such is the price of playing for a franchise with all those banners and retired numbers hanging from the rafters. They will not rest until they've talked to everyone, and I mean everyone: players, coaches, trainers, agents, even family members. Someone will, eventually, talk. I actually thought this kind of scrutiny was a good thing; it held us accountable.

The questions revolved around me this time. I hit only 12 of my 36 shots in four games, averaging barely over 10 points.

"What will you do to get Ray out of a slump?" they asked Doc.

My numbers were down, that much was true, but that was because of the double teams. In practice, as a matter of fact, we were running contingencies for every play, so I'd know where to throw the ball whenever they stuck another defender on me. I wasn't taking enough shots to be in a slump.

What got me angry was what Doc said.

"Ray will figure it out," he told the reporters. "We're not worried about Ray."

Doc was, in effect, agreeing with them. What he should've said was:

"Cleveland is taking Ray out of the offense, and we're doing everything we can to keep him involved. He doesn't need to score in this series."

When they asked me the same questions, I made the point about the lack of shots. That didn't please Doc, who had spoken to a former NBA coach he highly respected.

"He [the coach] read your comments," Doc told me, "and said I needed to tell you to stop talking to the newspapers, to keep the narrative on the team going forward."

Two days later, Doc asked me to come to his office.

"You have to be willing," he said, "to not score another bucket if that is what it takes for us to win a championship."

I told him I understood, although I wasn't sure it was such a good idea. They'd need me to score. If not this series, surely the next one, and if we went any further, the one after that.

One series at a time.

We won Game 5 in Boston but lost another Game 6, forcing another Game 7. In Games 5 and 6, I shot 7 for 19. Not especially impressive, I confess, but no slump either. So here we were again, one loss from being eliminated. Yet I wasn't antsy, as I had been going into Game 7 against the Hawks. I didn't send texts to my teammates in the middle of the night. Perhaps winning the first Game 7 so convincingly made me more confident about this one.

For much of the game, the Cavs, unfortunately, looked just as sure of themselves.

With two minutes left, they trailed by only one, 89–88, and had the ball. LeBron, with 44 points already, missed a three. We then scored on a jump shot by P. J. Brown, a backup forward we signed in February, to go up three. Delonte West, the Cavs' guard, missed a three, and on the next possession, LeBron missed from close range. That was basically it. The final: 97–92. Give credit to Paul, who matched LeBron with 41 points. As KG and I said, this was his team.

I scored just four points in Game 7. Slump or no slump, I needed to get on track. The Pistons, the winners of 59 games, were coming to town.

Which meant another duel with Richard Hamilton, a fellow UConn alum. People often compared him to me, the way he ran around screens to free himself for a shot. I liked Richard well enough, although he didn't get his nickname, "Rip," for no reason. He grew his nails two inches long on purpose, so if he was guarding you, you got bruises and scratches on your arms from him trying to get around a pick. I swear, when he shot a free throw, you could hear his nails scratching against the ball as it rolled up his fingers.

Rip, however, was a heck of a player, an integral member of the 2004 squad that beat the Lakers. Others remaining from that team—which made it to the Finals again in 2005, losing to the Spurs in seven—included Rasheed Wallace, Chauncey Billups, and Tayshaun Prince.

The Pistons knew how to win the big ones. We were still learning.

And I was still not where I needed to be.

In Game 1, I made just three of 10, scoring nine points. At least we got the victory, 88–79, thanks to KG, who had 26 points, nine rebounds, and two blocks; Paul added 22 points and six assists. In Game 2, I broke out, at last, going nine of 16, but Hamilton, Billups, Wallace, and their power forward, Antonio McDyess, were too good, and they prevailed, 103–97.

Headed to Detroit for the next two games, the pressure was definitely on. Few teams rally from being down three games to one.

Losing Game 2, as it would turn out, was the best thing that happened to us.

Before then, we didn't compete, away from Boston, with the sense of urgency we needed. Even though we didn't win one game in Atlanta or Cleveland, we still advanced to the conference finals. I wonder if, in the backs of our minds, we told ourselves: *We'll be okay if we lose on the road. All we have to do is take care of business at home and we'll win the series.* That wasn't the case any longer.

We didn't waste any time, capturing Game 3 handily, 94–80. KG was in superb form again: 22 points, 13 rebounds, and six assists.

Luck, I believe, also played a part. While I was warming up, I could tell something was wrong. The Palace, one of the loudest arenas in the league, was not nearly as rowdy as it should have been. The same night, the Red Wings, Detroit's beloved hockey team, were hosting Game 1 of the Stanley Cup Finals at the Joe Louis Arena. People's focus was divided. Hey, we'll take any advantage we can get.

Two nights later, the Pistons regrouped to defeat us, 94–75, and even the series, sending the teams back to Boston. In Game 5, the Garden as noisy as ever, I made five of six threes, scoring 29 points in a 106–102 victory. Perk also came through, with 18 points and 16 rebounds. We then rallied from 10 behind to take Game 6 in Detroit, 89–81, holding them to 13 points in the final quarter.

The journey up to this point hadn't been as smooth as we would have preferred, but we were where we wanted to be all along, in the Finals, and only the Lakers, the Celtics' top rival since the '60s, stood in the way. Our teams had met so many times in the Finals. It seemed fitting they were meeting again.

We believed in ourselves, even if others didn't seem to. The experts in the media made LA the favorite. We had lost three times to both the Hawks and the Cavaliers, while the Lakers lost three times to the Nuggets, Jazz, and Spurs *combined.* We couldn't care less what the experts said. If anything, it made us more motivated.

A friend told me months earlier: "You guys look good on paper. The only thing that will keep you from winning it all is an injury."

I thought of what he said the moment I saw Paul go down midway through the third quarter of Game 1 after colliding with Perk near the basket. He stayed on the floor for a long time, holding his right leg. Then he was carried to the locker room and put in a wheelchair, never a good sign. Yet we couldn't dwell on missing Paul. Not then. We had a game to win. The Lakers were up by four.

Leave it to Doc to keep us focused. Ubuntu. Of course.

"What did the guy from South Africa say about adversity?" Doc said in the huddle. "Nothing can get you down . . . adversity. You overcome it . . . nothing stops us. That's why we play 12 guys."

Not long afterward, the score then tied, the fans were on their feet. That's because Paul was coming through the tunnel and, like Superman, ready to go back in. We wound up with the victory, 98–88. Paul, who sprained his knee, had 22 points, 11 after returning from his collision with Perk. We limited the Lakers to 15 in the fourth. Kobe had 24, but was only nine for 26.

Doc was right. Defense is what will win us a championship.

Game 2 was the Leon Powe game. Leon, a six-foot-eight backup forward from Cal, scored 21 points in just 14 minutes. I always felt he was the most underrated player on our team, and it was a shame he was held back by knee problems for most of his career. The final: 108–102. We had done what we set out to do. California, here we come!

Going into Game 3 at the Staples Center, we were concerned. About the Lakers, naturally, who, in addition to Kobe, had Lamar Odom, Pau Gasol, and Derek Fisher.

Also about Paul.

Being from Los Angeles, he would stay at his home instead of the hotel and might drift away from the team. This was no time for that. We had to make sacrifices, Doc said. We had to be one. Now more than ever.

Paul ended up having a tough night—on the court. He scored six points, hitting just two of 14, and the Lakers won, 87–81, to avoid going down 3–0.

Even so, we didn't lose because of Paul. We lost because of Kobe, who scored 36, and Sasha Vujacic, their reserve guard, who had 20. Leon one game, Sasha the next. Forget about the starters. Perhaps this series would come down to which team had the better bench. Either way, we were still in a very good position. Steal the next one, and we'd put the Lakers in a deep hole.

Game 4 took place on June 12. I played 1,471 games during my professional career, including the postseason, and another 101 in college. No game means more to me than this one.

It sure did not start out very promising, except if you rooted for the purple and gold. The Lakers took a 21-point lead in the first quarter, were up by 18 at the half, and were still ahead, 70–50, with six minutes to go in the third.

You don't come back from a deficit that big. Not in the playoffs, and especially not on the road.

Doc used to tell us, whenever we were down by 20: "Let's

get it under 10, and we will turn it into a game." The other team, he said, will begin to feel the pressure and make mistakes.

We got it under 10, all right, and it took only four minutes: after Paul completed a three-point play, the score was 73–64. We had gone five of six from the field; the Lakers were just one of six. Scoring the final ten points of the quarter, we trailed by just two going into the fourth. Game on!

I knew one thing: no way was I coming out. Normally, Doc gives me a breather with about five minutes to go in the first quarter until early in the second. No breathers tonight. We couldn't afford to fall any further behind.

Yes, I was exhausted. In addition to running around screens to get my own shot, I guarded Kobe. Every time-out felt like the 60 seconds between rounds of a heavyweight championship bout. Get me the water, Gus. Put a towel on my head. Don't forget the mouth guard. Now send me out there for another round. *Ding!*

"If you need to come out, let me know," Doc said during a time-out in the fourth.

"No, I'm okay," I told him. "I got you."

"Good," he said, "because I need you to stay in."

A lot of my energy came from Shannon, my mom, and a few of the other wives and family members rooting for us behind the bench.

"Keep going, keep going," they said. "You guys got it!"

With just under five minutes to go, we went on an 8–0 run to assume a five-point lead. We were still ahead by three with 40 seconds left and had possession. One more basket just might do it.

The ball was in my hands near half-court, Sasha on me. He and I had been going at each other for the whole series.

He didn't play dirty, like Bruce Bowen, or scratch me, like Rip Hamilton. Sasha flopped, which I have zero respect for.

"Stop crying," I told him whenever he complained to the officials. He didn't stop.

The shot clock was winding down. At this point, a lot of people probably assumed I would wait until the very end and launch a three. I had another idea. To remind people I could go to the hoop as well as anyone.

I dribbled toward the top of the key, and there was plenty of room to maneuver. No help was coming. No screen for a pick-and-roll. Just Sasha and me.

One quick move to the right, and I was by him, just as I drew it up in my head. Gasol tried to stop me, but he was too late. I laid it in off the glass with my left hand. The lead was five. The game was over.

I couldn't believe it. We had really done it. We had come from 24 points down on their floor! The fans were stunned. Our guys were ecstatic.

When I got to the locker room, however, I didn't feel like celebrating. I felt like collapsing. I played hard game after game for 18 seasons, but this was the only game that, when the buzzer sounded, I had absolutely nothing left to give. It wasn't because I played the full 48 minutes, although I can't recall doing that before; it was because of everything in my career, and life, that had led me to that moment.

Little did I know that a much tougher challenge was yet to come, and that it would have nothing to do with basketball.

The whole week, our son Walker, who was 17 months old, wasn't himself. Based on his symptoms of throwing up and fatigue, we figured he had the flu. So we had a friend stay with him in the hotel on the night of Game 4.

He didn't get any better. Two days later, in the middle of the night, Shannon took him to a doctor who was on staff at the hotel. It looks like a virus, the doctor said, maybe food poisoning. But to be safe, he told her, go to the hospital and don't leave without a blood test.

Someone at the hospital didn't think he needed a blood test, but no one is more determined than Shannon. Thank God.

Twenty minutes later, the attending physician, white as a ghost, told her the news: "Your son has type 1 diabetes, and if he doesn't get insulin soon, you're going to lose him."

I was in my room—the players and their wives stayed at separate hotels—when she called. I'd heard of diabetes before, but only on those commercials you see on daytime TV. I knew nothing of what it does to a person, not to mention a little kid.

"Do you want me to come right now?" I asked.

"No," Shannon said, "go play your game, but when it's over, get your ass over here. I need you."

I got off the phone and went downstairs to the ballroom for the walk-through we have before every game, where Doc goes over the sets and plays we're likely to run. We usually have it at the arena where we'll be playing, but our hotel in Beverly Hills was a long drive from Staples. No sense in going back and forth. I always paid close attention in walk-throughs, never knowing when I might see something in our spacing that could make a difference.

Not this walk-through. My mind was on Walker and diabetes, on a future Shannon and I could never have imagined. I prided myself on being prepared for every scenario, but how did one prepare for this?

I didn't say a word to anybody until I arrived at Staples and spoke to Doc. He needed to know I wouldn't be my normal self. How could I be?

"I'm so sorry to hear that," he said. "We will get some people who can help you guys out. Your boy will be all right."

So I played, although not particularly well, as you might expect, hitting four of 13 in a 103–98 loss. The game is a blur to me. All I remember is looking over at my mother and a few friends every chance I could. Walker will be okay, they assured me. Would he? I never left an arena as fast as I did that night, and I didn't care if the writers thought I was skipping out because we lost. I couldn't wait to see my son. He was the only person who mattered.

There was so much to learn about the disease: how to give Walker the insulin, how to monitor his blood sugar, how to set up his diet. How to keep him alive.

One decision we had to make right away was what to tell people, if anything. Some of our friends thought we should keep the matter private. Shannon and I disagreed. We felt that going public might help others with kids who have diabetes. You would not believe how many die every year from being misdiagnosed. So, if any flu-like symptoms persist, do not hesitate to get a blood test.

The fact that our son was diagnosed while I was on the biggest stage of my career was no accident; it was the very stage we could use to save lives.

The organization back home was unbelievable. They arranged for a private jet to take us to Boston the next day, and they made sure we met with doctors at the Joslin Center, the top diabetes research facility in the world. The concern the

Celtics showed was something Shannon and I will always remember.

And oh, by the way, there was still Game 6 of the NBA Finals, the next biggest game of my life, to be played.

Some wondered, once word got around, if I would play. I certainly would, and mostly that was due to the amazing help we got for Walker. He was feeling good enough to sit on Shannon's lap during the entire game. Every time I looked over, I was reminded of how grateful I was that he wasn't taken from us.

So here we are. The game.

We traded baskets for the first quarter, and for the first five minutes or so of the second. Until we made our move.

A three by James Posey. A three by Eddie House. Two free throws by Eddie. Another three by James. The lead was suddenly 14 points, and by the half, 23.

Nonetheless, we didn't get ahead of ourselves. We came back from 20 down in their building, so there was no reason to think they couldn't come back from 20 down in ours. As usual, the key to maintaining a lead like that is to tell yourself the game is tied. It's not easy, human nature being what it is.

"The first shot you miss," we used to say, "is the first pass to the other team's fast break."

Whatever we told ourselves, it worked. After three quarters, we were up by 29. Now we just had to wait for the horn to let it all out.

The final: Celtics 131, Lakers 92. There would be another banner to hang with the others.

My emotions were all over the place that night, and for days to come. Too much had happened in the last year, in the last *week*, for them not to be.

I felt totally vindicated. After each season before, I'd watched other teams play for a title and felt unworthy, like I had cheated the ownership and the city I played for. They were paying me an obscene amount of money, but what, precisely, was I giving them in return? Not a championship. Not even a trip to the Finals.

Now, at last, I could sit home, think of the owners, and tell myself: "I did what you brought me here to do." In Game 6, I hit seven of nine threes to finish with 26 points.

I finally had an answer for the fans as well. Every summer I would hear the same question: "What happened to you guys this year?"

"Wait until next year," I would tell them, and believe me, I got sick of saying it.

I didn't leave the Garden until about four in the morning. At one point, Paul, KG, and I sat together in the locker room, no other players around. I don't recall what we said, but I recall how we felt. All those years of losing and now this.

And yet, as the days wore on, there was a part of me that felt empty, and it wasn't because Walker getting sick proved how little basketball meant compared to real life; I knew that already. It had more to do with having always believed that when you win a championship you're transported to some new, exalted place. What I realized was that you are the same person you were before, and that if you are not content with who you are, a championship, or any accomplishment, isn't going to change that.

My favorite part of winning the title wasn't hugging my

teammates, or watching the fans celebrate. It was standing on the podium with Walker in my arms. His eyes were red. He was tired. He had been through so much for someone so young, so little. But I knew he would be fine, and that we would take care of him.

A few days later, we went on the Duck Boat, this time as a championship team. I was blown away at how many people turned out to revel in the moment. Up in the high-rises and down in the alleys, in block after block, they were everywhere.

I thought back to the ride in October, when it was just Doc, Paul, KG, and myself.

When there was nothing more than a dream.

13

SO CLOSE, AND YET . . .

We pulled the ropes, sliding the banner into the place it would occupy forever.

Another opening night in Boston Garden. Another chance to celebrate.

The fans had been waiting since 1986 for the next banner to go up, and now that it had happened and another season was here, the question was: Could we do it again?

It would be a tougher task than winning it the first time, and that's true in every sport. The other teams, studying your blueprint for success, try to copy you. Then there's the challenge of how to manage your own expectations, as individuals and as a team. They're not the same as they were before. Michael Jordan put it best when I ran into him that summer. "You guys got lucky," he told me. "Winning one is lucky. Winning two, now you would be doing something."

I felt a little uncomfortable discussing the subject with MJ. I wasn't in his league. He had six championships; I had one. Still, I listened. How could I not?

"The major problem you're going to have to worry about is your role players not wanting to play their roles anymore," Michael went on. "They go home after the season, and everybody tells them how great they are, and it goes to their heads. They come back and want more minutes and more shots."

Only time would tell if that would happen to us.

Speaking of roles, I took on a new one myself that summer. The role of husband.

Shannon and I were vacationing on July 4 on Martha's Vineyard when the idea of getting married occurred to us. A month later, in front of about 40 friends and family, we said our vows. I fell in love that night at the All Star Café in New York, and the love was deeper than ever.

On opening night, we picked up our rings, sprinkled with diamonds and emeralds, and got back to work, knocking off Cleveland, 90–85. We did it without James Posey, who had signed a four-year contract with the New Orleans Hornets for $25 million. James would now have two rings to show his teammates.

Losing James, who could hit the three besides playing excellent defense, was a blow, but we still had our core and a strong bench—as we saw on opening night, when Leon Powe scored 13 points and Tony Allen added 11.

In mid-November, after a rare setback at home, to Denver, we went on a tear and didn't lose again until Christmas Day, to the Lakers in Los Angeles, the streak ending at 19, the longest in franchise history. We were 27-3, the same record we had at this point in the season before. Maybe Michael was wrong.

He wasn't.

Rondo, Perk, and Glen "Big Baby" Davis, a backup forward, demanded larger roles. There was absolutely nothing wrong with that, in my opinion. You want to have players with ambition. KG, Paul, and I had our max contracts and All-Star Game appearances. Far be it from us to tell them they shouldn't go after the same rewards.

Only having a larger role should happen naturally, in the flow of the offense. If, on a given night, depending on the matchups, that means fewer shots or less playing time, so be it.

Take Big Baby, who wanted more touches. When he got the ball, he often took shots before we were able to develop any kind of rhythm, and Doc had to sit him down. Perk also wanted more touches, and I tried to accommodate him— too much, apparently. Stop throwing the ball to Perk, Doc told me. As for Rondo, he was becoming one heck of a point guard, although he too was seeking a more prominent role, altering the dynamic that worked so well for us in 2008.

So, even though we were 41-9 in early February, on another streak at 12 wins and counting, I didn't have quite the same feeling about the direction we were heading in as I had the year before. No Ubuntu in this group. Too often we had to remind guys to move the ball around, instead of looking out for themselves. The final extra pass in each possession—no one did it better than the Spurs—is usually the one that gives you the best look at the basket. The pass we weren't making.

Then, two weeks later, it happened, what I feared most in 2008.

In a game against the Utah Jazz, KG hurt his leg going for an alley-oop. He had to sit out a few weeks. We hoped he'd be ready for the playoffs, but the grimace on his face whenever I saw him was not a very encouraging sign. We would have to defend our title without him.

Defending it began in earnest in a first-round matchup against the Bulls. You couldn't have asked for more suspense. Four of the games went to overtime, including an unbelievable Game 6 in Chicago. Up three games to two, we were looking to close them out.

I could not have played any better that night, scoring 29 points . . . in the first half! More than the rest of the team combined.

Nonetheless, we were trailing, 59–57. I went through a difficult stretch in the third quarter but, in the fourth, scored nine points on a 23–3 run that helped us rally from a 12-point deficit. I hit a 17-footer with about two minutes left to put us up by five, though the Bulls staged a comeback of their own to tie it at 101.

We called time. Twenty-nine seconds to go.

Doc drew up a play for Paul. In other circumstances, I would've had no problem with the call, since Paul was a sensational one-on-one player.

I had a problem this time. As hot as I was—I would finish with 51 points—I was the most logical choice to take the shot. Paul, conversely, was struggling; he would end up five of 13. We tried to get him going, but it was just one of those nights.

Whatever I was thinking, I kept my mouth shut. Remember when Scottie Pippen sat out the last 1.8 seconds of a playoff game in 1994 after Phil Jackson called for Toni Kukoc to take the final shot? Michael was playing baseball at the time. Taking himself out of the game is part of Scottie's legacy, and he has to live with it. Kukoc, by the way, hit the shot as the Bulls beat the Knicks.

Unfortunately, there was no happy ending for us.

Paul missed, and we lost in triple overtime, 128–127. I'm not saying I would have made the shot. You can never say that. Only that I liked my chances.

That loss hurt, and with one more, we'd be done. Yet, having been in this position the season before on two occasions and survived, we believed in ourselves—and came through again by defeating the Bulls in Game 7, 109–99. Eddie House went five for five, including four threes.

On to the conference semifinals against the Orlando Magic.

That was where not having KG was a killer. Big Baby tried his best. He even won a game for us, Game 4, hitting a jump shot at the buzzer to square the series. But he wasn't KG. He couldn't rotate over quickly enough to cover Hedo Turkoglu and Rashard Lewis, my former teammate in Seattle, on the perimeter. Rasheed and Turkoglu couldn't miss, and we never knew where the next shot was coming from.

In that series, by the way, their players did something I had never seen before. While they were in the layup line prior to tip-off, they danced and held a dunk contest. In the playoffs!

"They're taking this as a joke," I told the guys.

Joking around or not, the Magic blew us out in Game 7 at the Garden. So much for defending our title.

I don't like to make excuses, but I can't help but feel that if KG hadn't been injured, we would have come out of the East and met the Lakers, the eventual champions, in the Finals again. Man, that would have been fun.

Then, in 2009–10, came a season to remember. And an ending to forget.

We started out strong once again. Six in a row. Twenty of 24. Twenty-seven of 37. KG was his old self, while Rondo made plays at both ends of the court you don't see other point guards make. Even so, we went through some tough times beginning in mid-January. During one stretch, we dropped six of eight.

Doc, as usual, found a way to motivate us.

We were in the locker room at Staples, having just beaten the Lakers, 87–86, although there was no reason to get overly excited: Kobe didn't play.

"Guys, we're going to be back here," Doc told us, meaning the Finals. "I want each of you to give me $100, and we'll come back in June to collect."

Everyone contributed, including players, coaches, and team managers, bringing the total to a couple thousand. Doc put the cash in an envelope, got up on a chair, and hid it under one of the ceiling tiles.

"Obviously, you can't tell anyone," he said.

I thought it was brilliant. Coaching is about more than drawing up X's and O's and making the correct substitutions. Coaching is about having a certain mind-set, an unwilling-ness to surrender, and getting your players to fully buy in.

And now that we had invested in ourselves, we had to follow through.

A few weeks later, at a hotel ballroom in Cleveland, he was even more emphatic.

"This thing is doable," Doc said, showing us the schedule for the rest of the season. "Who in this conference can beat us? Which one of these teams you afraid of?" No one said a word.

He went on: "We're not going to get home-court advantage, so we'll have to win on somebody's floor to get a championship. Tell me if anyone in this room believes it's not doable."

Again, not a word. When Doc was finished, the guys were ready to storm the beaches at Normandy.

In the first round, we took care of the Heat in five games. So far so good. Then came LeBron and the Cavaliers, the number 1 seed in the East. Most people didn't give us a chance. Cleveland had won 61 games that season, 11 more than we did.

The Cavs took Game 1, 101–93. But thanks to 19 assists from Rondo, we squared the series in Game 2, only to give home-court right back when they beat us at the Garden by 29. That must have woken us up, as we captured the next three to win it in six.

The Magic were next. We got revenge for 2009, that series ending in six as well. Doc was right: this was doable. Only one test remained: the Lakers.

It promised to be quite a series.

When we arrived at Staples, there was something we needed to pick up before practice started. The cash hidden in the ceiling, of course. Doc shut the door.

"Everyone gather around," he said. "We're back here, just like we said we were going to be."

He stood on a chair, retrieved the envelope, and handed us our money. Now it was time to go after the real prize.

For me, Games 2 and 3 will always stand out, for vastly different reasons.

We needed Game 2 badly. In Game 1, the Lakers had defeated us, 102–89, Kobe with 30 points, seven rebounds, and six assists. Unless we took the next one, we'd fall behind two games to none, leaving little margin for error.

I was feeling pretty optimistic, being used to having good games against the Lakers, and against the Western Conference teams in general. The bigs in the West didn't defend the pick-and-rolls the way the bigs in the East did. They stayed in the paint. When I came off a pick, I would usually get a clean look at the basket. A shooter can't ask for anything more. Except, obviously, for the shots to fall in.

Which was what happened in Game 2. I scored 32 points, hitting eight of 11 threes in a 103–94 victory. Back to Boston we went. Win the three games there, and we'd hang another banner—one that, a few months before, no one could have seen coming.

First we had to win Game 3. We didn't, and that was on me.

The numbers were ugly enough—zero for 13, eight of which were threes—but it was my approach heading into the game that set me back. I figured the Lakers would defend me the way they defended me in Game 2. They didn't. Every time I came off a screen, somebody was in my face. They weren't going to let me go off for 32 again.

"Stay on Allen," Phil Jackson kept urging his guys. "Don't let him get open."

I should have done what I learned from George Karl and let the game come to me. Don't rush your shot. Try one from midrange. Give them a pump fake and drive into the lane. Get someone else a look. Anything but keep launching threes. Anything to take the Lakers out of their game plan and force them to adjust again. We lost 91–84, and LA was back in control.

Even so, I didn't get down on myself. You can't allow the lows to be too low or the highs too high in this game or, pardon the pun, you'll become a basket case.

Anyway, we bounced back to take Game 4, 96–89, Big Baby with 18 points off the bench, and went on to capture Game 5, 92–86, despite 38 from Kobe.

Returning to Los Angeles, I felt very good about our chances of winning Game 6, and another championship.

Until I saw Paul.

During our walk-through at the hotel, he was leaning against the wall and was not as dialed in as he should have been. I wasn't the only one who noticed.

"Paul, pay attention," Doc said. "I need you here."

That night, Paul scored 13 points and turned the ball over five times. To be fair, none of us were as dialed in as we should have been. The result: Lakers 89, Celtics 67. There was more sobering news. Perk injured his knee in the first quarter and didn't return. He would be declared out for Game 7.

So here we were, right where we were destined to be. One game to decide it all.

In the hours leading up to the game, I prepared like I always did. I got my shots up, and the proper rest, and tuned out any distractions. Doc, for a change, didn't say anything to motivate us, and he shouldn't have had to. If you're not motivated for the most important game of the series—of the *season*—well, that's on you.

We got off to a strong start, leading 23–14 after the first quarter. The lead was six at halftime. Then, beginning the third quarter, we went on a 9–2 run to go ahead 49–36. In a low-scoring game such as this, each possession a struggle, 13 points was a big advantage.

By the end of the quarter, however, it was only four. Kobe wasn't having one of his better nights—he would end up six for 24—but Ron Artest, the Lakers' small forward, was all over the place, scoring baskets, making steals, firing up his teammates and the fans.

With six and a half minutes to go, I hit two free throws to put us on top, 64–61. It would be our last lead of the night.

Lakers 83, Celtics 79.

After congratulating the Lakers, I couldn't get to the locker room quickly enough. I wasn't going to stick around and watch them celebrate.

Once everyone was together, Doc got our attention.

"You had a great year, guys," he said. "You can hold your heads high."

He told us to form a circle one last time.

Forming a circle is a big deal in basketball, as I'm sure you've noticed with other teams. With us, Doc used to say: "Everybody, come in and touch someone." One player, and it was usually KG, stood in the middle and said a few inspiring words. The message was unmistakable: we are a team, and no one person is more important than another.

This was one circle I shall never forget. Rasheed Wallace, the ex-Pistons forward/center we signed as a free agent before the season, who was one of the toughest guys in the league, was in tears.

"You guys were great," Rasheed said. "I appreciate everything that you did. I'm glad I could go on this journey with you." Although he had a year left on his contract, he told us right then he was retiring. He had nothing left to give. I knew how he felt.

I went dark for the next week. Or it might have been two weeks; I wasn't keeping track. I sat by myself in a room at our home in Boston and did nothing but watch TV. I wasn't interested in going anywhere or talking to anyone—about Game 7, or any game.

You'd think I would have had a broader perspective by this point, after what Shannon and I went through with Walker and after realizing that winning a championship doesn't change who you are.

But it is still quite an accomplishment, and it had been in our grasp—until it was gone.

Our window was closing, especially once LeBron took his talents to South Beach and teamed up with Dwyane Wade and Chris Bosh to form a Big Three of their own. They were now the talk of the NBA.

Only our window was not closed yet.

In the 2010–11 season, we took 23 of our first 27, including 14 straight, before losing to the Magic, 87–78, on Christmas Day. We still had our core from 2008, and had replaced Rasheed with another vet with championship experience: Shaquille O'Neal.

In early February, we went to meet the Bobcats in Charlotte, where I would have a chance to break the record for most three-pointers, held by Reggie Miller with 2,560; I was only three behind. To be honest, I felt uneasy with the attention I was getting from the media. Basketball is a team sport. I never set out to break any records, this one included.

It was too late. The record would soon be mine, and that being the case, I wanted to break it in Boston, not Charlotte. So that night—I'm not proud to admit this—I made sure not to break the record. On several possessions, when I was open for a three, I took my sweet time, came in a couple of steps, and opted for a two instead. I attempted only two three-pointers the entire game, nailing both, leaving me one back of Reggie.

A few nights later, at home against the Lakers, I hit a three late in the first quarter to set the new mark. Speaking of Reggie, he was doing the color commentary for TNT that night, and after breaking the record I went over to give him a hug.

In Denver two weeks later, I was standing near the free-throw line next to Birdman—you know, Chris Andersen, the tall white dude with the colorful tattoos all over his body.

"Man, I watched the game the other night. That was cool," he said, referring to me passing Reggie.

What Chris said really affected me. As a player, you become so wrapped up in your own world, you forget that the other players in the league are fans too.

One thing I didn't lose sight of was my relationship with Rajon Rondo. It had been pretty bad for some time.

Back in 2009, when I was told the two of us might be traded to the Phoenix Suns, I called to let him know the word was that he and Danny Ainge didn't get along and that was why there was talk of a deal.

"You need to meet with Danny," I told Rondo, "to iron out any issues you guys might have."

I don't know if he ever did speak to Danny, but, obviously, the deal wasn't made. Later, though, Rondo brought the matter up before practice. He brought up a lot of things.

"I carried all of you to the championship in 2008," he blurted out.

The rest of the team, almost in unison, responded, "You *what*?"

"Each one of you had issues with me," Rondo said.

"None of us had issues with you," I chimed in.

"You did too," he said, looking directly at me. "You told me I was the reason we were going to be traded."

"I never said that, Rondo. I was just telling you what I heard."

On and on it went, and nothing that I said, or anyone said, got through to him. He believed what he wanted to believe. There was no question about Rondo's talent. His ability to be a leader was a whole other issue.

Leaders work hard, day after day, not just on days when 15,000 people happen to be watching. Leaders also don't put their own stats ahead of the team. There were times when Rondo would pass up a sure layup in order to pick up an assist; that was the record he was going for.

"Dude, lay it up," I would tell him. "You're just trying to pad your assists total."

Doc noticed what was happening and tried to find a

solution. One day, in 2010 or 2011, he asked KG, Paul, and me to come to his office. He got right to the point.

"You guys have to let him into the circle," he said. "You have to give him a voice."

KG and I couldn't have disagreed more.

"We can't make him a leader," I told Doc. "He has to earn it."

The days of being Rondo's mentor were long gone. I had become his enemy at some point, and I would be his enemy for the rest of my days in Boston.

That had never been my intention, as it wasn't with George Karl, or anyone I didn't get along with. And even if I wasn't the best of friends with another player, he was still my teammate and I wanted to do whatever I could to help him.

That included Rajon Rondo. He had problems from the line, hitting less than 60 percent. Most games are lost by eight points or fewer, and teams miss about ten free throws a game. If Rondo could raise his percentage to, say, 70 percent, even 65, that could be a huge boost for us.

One day before practice, I saw my opportunity.

"Let's shoot some free throws together," I suggested.

Rondo didn't say a word, but the look on his face said enough: *I don't need your help.*

I walked away and never offered to work with him again. I can't help somebody who doesn't want to help himself. Frankly, it made no sense to me. Here was a chance to get advice from one of the better free-throw shooters in the game. How can you *not* take it?

In 2011, during our playoff series against the Heat, we saw Rondo's anger like never before. We were at practice the day after losing Game 2 in Miami to fall behind 2–0. Yet Doc, it should come as no surprise, was as upbeat as ever.

"I want you guys to watch this film," he said. "We're not that far from what we need to do. We did a few things to beat ourselves."

He proceeded to show us what they were: The layups we missed. The defenders we didn't box out. The switches we didn't make. One clip showed Rondo failing to get back on defense.

"Rondo, look at your body language," Doc said.

Rondo didn't say a word and stopped looking at the screen. He put his head down and turned his chair toward the lockers.

"Bro, watch the film," Doc told him.

"Fuck that film," Rondo said as he stood up and threw a water bottle that cracked the screen. The rest of us got up too, thinking Rondo was going to charge Doc. That's how much of a rage he was in.

"Get him out of here," Doc said.

Rondo took off, KG right behind him, practice done for the day. KG, you had to figure, being the no-nonsense, team-first guy he was, was going to tell him to wise up. Whenever somebody kidded around too much on the bench or in the locker room, he'd set him straight. Such as one of the times Rondo came to a shootaround with his shoes untied, the laces out, his hands in his pants.

"Young fella," KG said, "you need to get your shit together."

He didn't tell Rondo off this time. Just the opposite.

"Youngun, you're going to be all right," he said.

If KG wouldn't keep him in line, we were in trouble.

Because Paul certainly wouldn't get involved. "I'm just gonna do my time," he used to say.

Nor did Doc really try, though there were occasions, besides the incident at practice, when it looked like the two were about to trade blows. One evening, I was in my hotel room when I got a call from Doc. "Let's go to dinner," he said. It wound up being Doc, KG, and myself. Paul was invited too, but didn't make it.

"We can't win with Rondo; he's not a good dude," Doc told us. "I spoke to the ownership, and they're on board for him to be traded."

KG didn't defend him. He knew Rondo had to go.

He didn't go.

The trade discussed would have sent Rondo to the New Orleans Hornets for their exceptional point guard Chris Paul, but in the end Doc decided he couldn't do that to their coach, Monty Williams. Doc was a mentor to Monty, having coached him in Orlando.

So imagine my reaction in the 2011–2012 season when it became increasingly clear that Rondo wasn't going anywhere. And since they could not trade him, the thinking was, they might as well find a way to make this work.

That season, my last under contract, was the most stressful by far. It got to the point that Rondo would not even throw the ball to me. I would be wide open coming off a screen and he'd go in another direction.

"What's up with your boy?" my friends asked me.

Not wanting to start any rumors, I'd respond: "Oh, he sees something better."

Behind the scenes, however, I complained to Doc.

"Yeah, me and the coaches talked about it," he said. "We've

got to figure out something to do." His idea was to bring me off the bench for Rondo so that I would play alongside another guard, Avery Bradley, who was in his second season.

"You'll get more touches," Doc said.

Why, I wondered, didn't he just tell Rondo what he expected from him? Wasn't that his job?

"Trust me," Doc used to say all the time, "I know what I'm doing. I've been a part of the NBA for more than 25 years."

"Doc, I've been in the NBA almost half of my life too," I finally said to him once. "Just because you say this is how it's supposed to be done doesn't mean it's the only way."

Now, you can see why the Celtics might want to get rid of me, and at one point it looked like they had done just that. The call came from Danny right before the deadline, in March: "Ray, you have been traded to Memphis." For O. J. Mayo, their young shooting guard.

I called home right away. Shannon, as usual, took the news in stride. If I had been dealt to the moon, she would have said, "No problem," and gone to look for her astronaut suit. I never took trades well, as you know. For once, at least, I didn't hear the news first from the media.

It didn't matter. Danny called back to say the deal was off. I never did find out what happened. Nonetheless, as long I was still in Boston, I was determined to make the most of it.

The season did not start until Christmas Day, because of another owner lockout, and was reduced to 66 games. It was a struggle the first two months. In one stretch, we lost seven of eight. But, in late March, we won seven of eight, including a victory over LeBron and the Heat, to put us at 30-22.

About a week later, we beat the Pacers on the road. You

would think, as a unit, that we were bonding at just the right time. Far from it, I'm afraid.

In Indiana, Paul and Brandon Bass, our other starting forward, were arguing with each other the entire game. I don't recall what started it, only that Paul was speaking to Brandon as if he were some kid, not a grown man.

"Talk to me with respect," Brandon kept insisting.

When I walked into the locker room after the game, they were still at it, and it looked like they were about to throw punches.

"Guys, what about Ubuntu?" Doc said.

"Man, we ain't been Ubuntu in here all year," Rondo said.

"What are you talking about?" Doc responded.

Then, Rondo, out of nowhere, brought my name up. I had been sitting there, icing my feet, trying to stay out of it. So much for that idea.

"What the hell are you talking about?" I said as I leaped up.

"You're jealous of me," Rondo went on.

"Jealous of you? For what? You need to stop bullshitting everyone on the team," I told him, "and play every night instead of when you choose to play."

The two of us were now screaming at each other, Rondo acting as if he thought he were the GM as well as the point guard.

"I'm going to get your ass out of here this summer," he vowed.

"Dude, I'm going to be gone before you have any say-so. I'm out of here."

That was the end of it. Until we were on the plane to Boston. I got out of my seat and approached Rondo, who had been chatting with Doc. I still felt that Rondo and I, as two adults, could resolve this, and with just three weeks to go before the playoffs started, we needed to.

"What makes you think I'm jealous of you?" I asked him.

"I'm good," he said.

"What do you mean, you're good?"

"I got 11 games to play with you, and that's it."

There was no point in saying another word. Whatever was between Rondo and me could not be resolved.

Somehow, we won eight of those 11 games to finish 39-27, setting up a first-round playoff series against the Hawks.

We lost Game 1 in Atlanta, 83–74, as Josh Smith had 22 points and 18 rebounds, but that wasn't what disturbed me the most about that day. With 41 seconds to go, Rondo was signaled for a technical after the official called a foul on Brandon. No big deal. We were trailing by four at that point and would have needed quite a rally to pull it out.

But then Rondo bumped the official, Marc Davis, with his chest. Huge deal. The NBA would take a close look and decide whether to suspend him.

Having missed the game due to an injury, I did an interview on the court afterward, and then went to the locker room. The guys were talking about the bump.

"Shorty," Paul told Rondo, "you don't need to say anything to the media. Just get dressed and get on the bus." KG agreed with Paul.

"He has to say something," I told them. "He has to own up to what he did."

Paul and KG didn't buy it for a second. I appealed to Rondo, for practical reasons, if nothing else.

"Tell them your adrenaline was going and you didn't mean to bump him," I said. "You're already suspended. The question is, for how long? If you walk out, it shows no respect, that you don't give a damn."

He didn't buy it either. I wasn't surprised. He had never apologized, after all, for breaking the TV screen, and that was an important practice for us.

I approached Doc next.

"You need him to speak to the media or we're going to lose him for more than two games," I said.

Doc agreed, and Rondo gave in.

Fortunately, Rondo, as it turned out, was suspended only for Game 2, which we won anyway to square the series. We took the next two in Boston and closed the Hawks out in six.

Next was a date with the Philadelphia 76ers, who extended us to seven games. In Game 7, Rondo was the hero with 18 points, 10 assists, and 10 rebounds. When he played like that, we could beat anyone. And we would need him to play like that, as we'd be taking on LeBron James and the Heat in the Eastern Conference finals. We weren't intimidated, that's for sure.

Dropping the first two games in Miami didn't lessen our confidence one bit. In Game 2, as a matter of fact, we were up 11 in the third quarter before LeBron and D-Wade went off. Even then, we staged a comeback of our own to force overtime. Check out Rondo's stat line: 44 points, 10 assists, eight rebounds. By the way, he played the entire 53 minutes!

Sure enough, we won the next three, including Game 5 in Miami, 94–90, to grab a 3–2 lead. One more, and we were going back to the Finals.

In Game 6, however, LeBron poured in 45 as the Heat

beat us by 19 at the Garden. What I recall most about that night were people chanting, "Let's go, Celtics!" as the game was about to end. They were doing whatever they could to get us geared up for the *next* game—Game 7 in Miami. Like I said, you won't find better fans anywhere.

We were geared up, all right, the game tied at 73 heading into the fourth quarter. But the Heat pulled away to win, 101–88.

Yet, as disappointed as we were, there was nothing to be ashamed of.

No, the shame came after the game.

In the final seconds, I reminded the guys to congratulate Miami and wish them well in the Finals against Oklahoma City. You've seen it many times, the players hugging their opponents afterward, like boxers after a fight.

You didn't see it this time. Not from all my teammates.

"Screw those motherfuckers," one guy said, and he was not the only player who felt that way. "I'm not shaking anybody's hand."

I tried to talk them out of it, but they kept walking away.

We were no different from the Pistons team, who, about to be swept by the Bulls in the 1991 playoffs, headed to the locker room before Game 4 was over. That will always be a part of their legacy as much as the titles they won, and now I was afraid that failing to congratulate the Heat would be a part of ours. You find out a lot about an individual, or a team, in victory. You find out a lot more in defeat.

The Heat went on to beat the Thunder in five games for its first title with LeBron. Their future was as promising as ever. Our future wasn't. We had delayed the inevitable for a while but couldn't delay it any further. When the clock struck midnight on Sunday, July 1, for the second time in my career, I became a free agent.

The phone rang at 12:01. It was someone from the Memphis Grizzlies. This was going to be an interesting couple of weeks.

14

THE FINAL MOVE

The plan was to stay in Boston. There is no place like it. I knew it the first day, in July 2007, when my family and I arrived from Seattle for the press conference at the Garden.

One look at the practice facility and I thought: *Now, this is a franchise.*

To stay, however, I'd need to believe that the organization respected me. In a few weeks, I'd turn 37, old in NBA years. Earlier in my career, I figured to play about 12 years; that would be all my body could handle. I was at 16 years and counting. So, as long as the team did right by me, I would be back.

Except the Celtics were in no hurry to get anything

done. My agent kept reaching out to Danny, but he was put off each time as the team focused on coming to terms with everybody else. That included a player who wasn't even on the roster, free agent guard Jason Terry.

Finally, when they got around to me, their offer was $12 million for two years, far less than what I deserved, based on what other players around the league with my skill set were earning. I had asked for $24 million over three years, a sizable pay cut from the $10 million per season I'd been making—and $3 million less, incidentally, than Steve Nash would get the very next day from the Lakers. And he was a year older than me!

But the Celtics wouldn't move an inch from $12 million.

"I'm sorry, Ray, but this is all we can give you," Danny said.

Of course, a contract is usually about more than money, and this was no exception. I wanted some assurance of the role I'd have going forward. I had been gradually phased out of the offense and feared it would only get worse. Instead of throwing the ball to me or to Paul in the final seconds of a quarter, Rondo would dribble forever, and then launch a desperate three. Our efficiency at the end of quarters was horrible, and Danny knew it.

"I wish I could say you weren't telling the truth," he said.

I asked him to find out if there was reason to believe anything would be different next season.

"I'll take it to Doc," he told me, "and see what he has to say."

It didn't take long to get an answer.

"Doc said nothing is going to change," Danny said. "The offense is going to go through Rondo, and you need to be on board with it and win on this team's terms. If you're not, then you need to choose elsewhere."

So let me see if I got this straight:

You want to pay me less money. You want to bring me off the bench. You want to continue to run the offense around Rondo. Now tell me again exactly why I would want to sign this contract?

I got off the phone and texted KG.

"It's not looking like I'm going to be back with the team," I wrote. "Danny's not giving me the money."

"Nah, it's going to be all right," he texted back. "They're going to take care of you."

"No, he's not."

KG and I could have gone back and forth for hours, but there was no point. I knew what I knew, and since the Celtics were not going to take care of me, I realized my years in Boston were probably over.

Yet it took a call from my sister Kim to convince me to give up any last ray of hope. "You've made enough money in your career," she told me. "They're not respecting you. You haven't been happy for a long time. You've got to leave."

Kim was right. I needed to explore other options, which I was fortunate to have.

Miami was one. I would listen to what they had to say, but I had my doubts, still hurt from losing to them in the playoffs. Minnesota was another; how ironic, to be pursued by the team that drafted me in 1996 and then got rid of me 30 minutes later. Memphis, where I nearly went before the trade deadline, was also very interested, as it proved with the 12:01 AM call.

The team I was most intrigued by was the Los Angeles

Clippers, with their talented core of Chris Paul, Blake Griffin, and DeAndre Jordan. I made plans to stop in LA after first meeting with the Heat representatives in Miami. The Clippers were worried, however, that I was using them to get a better deal somewhere else. So I reached out to their coach, Vinny Del Negro.

"My ties in Boston are being severed," I assured him. "I've been treated unfairly. I am not using you guys for leverage. I'm trying to figure out the next place to go."

I don't know whether he believed me or not, but while in Miami, I found out the Clippers reached an agreement with another shooting guard, Jamal Crawford. So much for going there. It was now down to Miami, Memphis, and Minnesota. The Heat offered $6 million over two years, even less than Boston, while the Grizzlies and Timberwolves could propose no more than the $5 million–per-season midlevel exception. If this process were to go on for much longer, I'd be playing for free.

In the end, I chose Miami, and for one simple reason: the Heat afforded me the best chance to win a championship. Memphis had made the playoffs the last two years but failed to get past the second round, while Minnesota had not been in the postseason since 2004.

I knew fans in New England wouldn't be happy with my decision, but I never could have imagined the degree of unhappiness. They acted as if I was Benedict Arnold, and they weren't alone.

"Am I wrong," a player from another team tweeted, "for thinking ray allen is a traitor for signing with his rival team the heat?"

Yes, he was, but it did not matter what I thought. Once it was out there, others picked up on the same theme.

The criticism was unfair, and let me explain why.

First, Boston and Miami were not rivals. So the Heat beat the Celtics two straight years in the playoffs? You need more than two years to establish a rivalry. Secondly, it wasn't as if I was going for more money. I was taking *less* money.

My only sin was that I had the nerve to leave on my own. Some of the people who had wanted me out in the past were now the same ones furious with me for going. A cable TV station in town had done a poll a couple of years earlier, asking fans which player should be traded. Care to guess who received the most votes? I called the head of the station to complain.

"Why are you doing this?" I asked. "My family is watching. They're very hurt by this."

In any case, I felt then, and still feel today, that I have nothing to apologize for.

Okay, that's not entirely true. I regret not calling Paul before the news became official. I owed him that much after everything we had been through the past five years. Unlike KG, who knew how frustrated I was over my talks with Danny, Paul was totally in the dark. In my defense, however, things happen so fast when you're a free agent and trying to decide on your future.

A lot was made over KG refusing to acknowledge me a few months later when we opened the season against the Celtics in Miami. Others near the bench shook my hand and wished me well. Doc gave me a hug. KG acted as if I didn't exist.

Was I hurt? How could I not be? Was I shocked? Absolutely not.

KG would have snubbed his grandmother if she signed with another team. Perhaps it was too soon, the emotions too raw. I hope one day we have that talk we should've had at the steakhouse.

I will never forget what he said to me my first year in the league, his second. Our teams were playing each other in the preseason:

"Can you believe it? Look where we are."

Now I was going south, to another franchise, hoping to hold on to that feeling of awe and appreciation. Before this career I loved came to an end.

I arrived in Miami a battered dog, as I like to put it, from those last two seasons in Boston. I found it hard to believe I wasn't still there, fighting the same losing battles. My new teammates helped me get past all that, with the respect they showed me and one another.

You almost wouldn't know that these guys had won it the year before. The role players didn't show up at camp expecting more touches, more minutes . . . more everything. Veterans such as Shane Battier, Mike Miller, and James Jones were in the gym by the time I got there. Mike and James got up more shots than I did, and no one ever got up more shots than I did.

The tone, no surprise, was set by LeBron. I was impressed by his talent, but more by his desire to learn from others. He didn't assume he knew everything. Plenty of great players do, which keeps them from ever being greater. Shooting free throws was a perfect example. LeBron had his troubles from the line, and he'd be the first to admit it.

"We need to shoot free throws," he said to me one day. "I need you to tell me what I'm doing." I was glad somebody wanted my help. That had not always been the case in recent years.

"You want to focus from the start," I told him, "to get your percentage as high as you can. When you miss a few, you'll still be in the 80s, not the 70s. Get down in the 70s and it's hard to claw your way back." I got him to work on a new routine, but when he missed a few, he would drift back to his old routine, where he kept the basketball to one side of his body before letting it go.

"Don't worry," I told LeBron. "You can put the perfect stroke on a ball and have the perfect form and still miss. Now you just got to go and get the next one."

I was also impressed by his ability to recall everything that took place in a game, and not only the games he was in. He used to tell me details about the games *I* was in, ones I had forgotten long ago: how many points I scored, which players were on the floor, what plays our team ran down the stretch.

Perhaps what I admired most, though, was how often he gave credit to others.

"You guys were incredible," he said, referring to the teams I was on in Boston. "Paul was tough."

I couldn't believe it. Where I came from, if you said anything positive about a player on the other team, you were seen as a sucker. I always appreciated what my opponents could do, even if it came at my expense. Like me, they had made it this far for a reason.

LeBron saw himself as one of the guys, and that's rare for someone of his stature. The stars usually feel the need to separate themselves from everybody else, which is bad for team morale. I don't care if you average 25 points a night or play 25 minutes a week. If you're on the team, you're an equal. If you think you're better than us, we have a problem.

Yet, as devoted as he was, he knew how to have a good time. We'd arrive at the hotel, and I'd no sooner have put my bags down when the phone would ring.

"Meet me in my room," he'd say. "We're ready to play cards."

Count me in, I told LeBron, though I typically didn't stay for the whole time. The games, on occasion, went on until two or three in the morning, and as the old guy in the group, I needed my rest now more than ever. "I'll be sick in the morning if I don't go to sleep," I told them.

That's where their maturity made such a difference. They didn't hold it against me if I didn't spend every minute of my free time with them.

It wasn't like that in Boston. If I chose to stay home and not go out to a club with everyone else, I wasn't one of *them*. It didn't occur to them that I had five kids at home, four under the age of seven, and that Shannon and I were up at least once a night to keep track of Walker's blood sugar. Some nights we had to take him to the hospital. It was our new normal, and sleep was rare indeed. I got my best sleep on road trips, though I felt guilty Shannon had to stay up on her own.

Being a member of a team—and it can be a law firm, a club in school, a church choir, you name it—can be a tough balancing act. For somebody who sees himself as coming

246

from the outside, it's even tougher. The key is to make sure the others know you are on their side while, at the same time, remaining true to who you are and to what matters to you.

So if they ask you to go out and you can't, they won't say, "What the heck is wrong with you? The whole team's going." Instead, they will say, "Ray is with us. He just has stuff to do, and we understand."

I was also content on the court. This wasn't Boston circa 2007; I wasn't part of the Big Three this time. I was looking forward to the challenge, to be honest, to see the game in a way I hadn't seen it since freshman year at UConn. Just like back then, I still felt that the bench could be as important as the starters.

Coming off the bench has its drawbacks, though. You can't ease your way in, as you do when you're a starter. You have to catch up in a hurry to the rhythm of the game, and every game is different.

Your body also needs to be in the right place, and that's where the Heat could have managed the situation a little better. They ran us ragged, treating us as if we were the youngest team in the league when we were, in fact, one of the oldest.

In Boston, shootarounds lasted 40 minutes, sometimes 45. Get some plays down, get some shots up, and get the heck out of there. I would be showered, go home and then have a nap by 11:45.

In Miami, shootarounds lasted about two hours. I said something about it out loud once and had to catch myself:

"Damn, how long are we going to be out here?"

The coaches put us through drill after drill, as if we were back in high school trying out for the varsity. We then had to hurry home, get some rest, and be back for a game that night. That was a lot for a body to absorb in one day. I have nothing against shootarounds on game day; you need them. But what you need even more is for guys to be at their best, mentally and physically, when the horn sounds.

"Why didn't you tell me it was going to be like this?" I asked a teammate I'd known for a while.

"I really wanted to," he said, "but I just couldn't. I wanted you to come here."

Look, no place is perfect; I'd been around long enough to know that. Erik Spoelstra never played in the league, like Doc did for so many years. So he didn't have the same sense of how we, as older players, might feel deep into the season.

I was more nervous than usual on opening night, and not only because we were playing the Celtics. How they felt about me leaving was actually the least of my concerns after I signed with Miami. Anybody who has moved to another city to take a new job knows what I mean. You worry about finding a school for your kids and a neighborhood to live in; those are your priorities.

I was nervous about the fans. This would be their first time seeing me in a game that mattered, and they would judge me like fans in any city—with no sentimentality. Was it a smart move to sign me? Would I accept my role? Could the old man still play?

With just under three minutes left in the first quarter, I checked in and the fans gave me a very warm ovation. No, this would never be Boston, but the folks in Miami always treated me well. A minute later, I made the first shot I took, a three-pointer, and finished with 19 points. So much for nerves. We beat the Celtics, 120–107, and went on to win 12 of our first 15.

Going into the game against the Pacers on February 1, we were 29-13. They won easily, 102–89, evening our record on the road to 11-11. We needed to do better, and we did.

Two days later, we knocked off the Raptors in Toronto. Then, back home, Charlotte. Then the Rockets, the Clippers, the Lakers, and so on. We didn't lose again the rest of the month and for the first three weeks of March. Defeating the Magic on March 25 made it 27 straight, the longest streak in the league since 1972, when the Lakers won 33 in a row.

While others were talking about our chance to break the record, I don't remember it being on our minds too much. Getting a ring, that was all we cared about.

Sure enough, two nights later, the Bulls pulled off the upset, 101–97, in Chicago. You could see it coming. For some teams, the challenge of beating us—and ending the streak—was something to get up for in a season that was already lost. We finished 66-16—the same record, ironically, the Celtics posted my first year in Boston.

Our first opponent in the postseason was the Bucks, who hadn't won a playoff series since I was traded in 2003. We swept them in four, winning each game by double digits. I felt bad for Senator Kohl, who sold the team a year later.

Next up were the Bulls. Thanks to their explosive guard, Nate Robinson, who had 27 points and nine assists, they beat us, 93–86, at home. But we regrouped to capture Game 2 by 37 and proceeded to take the next three.

Then came the Pacers. We were fortunate to escape with Game 1, LeBron making a layup at the buzzer in overtime. We weren't fortunate in Game 2: the Pacers prevailed by four.

Winning at home was almost automatic for us during the regular season (37-4). That wasn't true any longer.

But, thanks to 17 points and seven rebounds from Udonis Haslem, in his 10th year with the team, we took Game 3 in Indiana, and won the series in seven.

I was back in the Finals, for the third time in six seasons. Not once did I take it for granted. Remember, I didn't make a single appearance in my first *11* years. When we lost Game 7 to the Sixers in 2001, I was confident I'd get there before too long.

It took seven years.

Standing in our way were the Spurs, who had not won a championship since 2007. That's a drought for that franchise. What always struck me, besides their unselfishness, was how they kept the core of Tim Duncan, Tony Parker, and Manu Ginobili together season after season.

Game 1 was in Miami, and again, we couldn't get it done, San Antonio winning, 92–88, despite another great performance from LeBron: 18 points, 18 rebounds, 10 assists. Duncan was also at his best: 20 points, 14 rebounds, three blocks. Game 2 was now an absolute must, and the guys came through, 103–84.

Texas, here we come.

We should have stayed home. The first half of Game 3 wasn't too bad—the Spurs led, 50–44—but the second half couldn't have been worse. They outscored us, 63–33.

It was our turn in Game 4.

We went on a 16–6 run during the fourth quarter to

break things open and get back in the series, the Big Three combining for 85 points, 30 rebounds, and 10 steals, six by D-Wade. The Spurs took Game 5, 114–104, to go up 3–2, but we had managed to get out of Texas alive and if we could win the next two in Miami, the title would be ours.

Game 6, as you would expect, was intense from the opening tip. The Spurs were up by six at the half and extended the lead to 10 after three quarters. Then, we went on a 17–7 run, tying it at 82 with six and a half minutes left. On the next possession, I hit my first hoop of the night for our first lead since late in the second quarter. *Nice of you to drop by, Ray.*

Down the stretch, neither team was able to take control. With about a minute and a half to go, Parker tied it with a three.

Then came the three straight turnovers, the Spurs now ahead by five, setting the stage for the final, unforgettable 28.2 seconds.

Time-out Heat.

What did Spoelstra say in the huddle? I can't remember, although I doubt we set up a play. Most times that season, in critical possessions, the plan out of a time-out was the same: give the ball to number 6.

Mike Miller, as you may recall, threw it to LeBron, who missed the first three but nailed the second after Mike got the loose ball. Then came the free throw from Kawhi Leonard to put San Antonio up by three.

Mario Chalmers, our point guard, brought the ball up the full length of the court. It was no secret LeBron was going to take the shot. Still, I was ready.

So what if I had just two points the whole night? In the

Big East championship game against Georgetown, I'd missed my previous 14 shots when Coach Calhoun called a play for me in our final possession. All it takes is one.

You know the rest: I made the three, we won Game 6 in OT, and Game 7 two nights later.

What a difference a year makes. One year I'm struggling for playing time and respect. The next, I'm drinking champagne and riding in another parade.

People always want to know which title means more to me, and the truth is, they both mean a great deal. Though after what I had to endure in Boston, there was a sense of vindication in 2013 that I didn't experience in 2008. I felt that going to Miami was the right decision. The championship confirmed it.

Even so, just like in 2008, winning it all didn't change my life.

I got to sleep around five in the morning after Game 7, but I was up by eight. I thought right away of the tasks I had put off for months, such as going to the dentist. I called to see if they could squeeze me in.

"You just won a championship," the receptionist said. "Shouldn't you be on a yacht somewhere partying?"

By nine, I was in the chair, getting work done on a filling.

Sure, I could have waited a few days, but that has never been my approach in basketball or in life.

Win a game, you should savor the moment, but don't get too excited; you have to prepare for the next one. So that morning, with no games left, meant seeing the dentist. That

LeBron was still at the to|re as ugly as the scores indi-
D-Wade. Plus, the bench w07–86 in Game 4.

In early March, we beatfficient coming out of a time-
to 43-14, although Spoelstra high-percentage shot every
and we always knew the te stars who beat us; they got
slump away from getting mds Danny Green and Patty

The slump came all righiful end in Game 5, 104–87,
by four losses in the next fiv boards.
to address the team. We saway. I was one for eight, the
junior high phys ed class. es to go in the first quarter.
Whatever it was, I'm sure h
got back to the level we weafterward. We didn't expect
the season 54-28.   e games. I sat in the locker

No matter. Knowing th shaking his head.
there was little to play for. Edecision to make—whether
People always used to tell whole sporting world would
the NBA."

I would never disagredon't have to tell you, would
also a job, and every job ge decide.

In any case, once the plavs, I knew I would not be
team. No longer were we flyon was: Would I follow him
staying up all hours of the b convince me, and I think
pursuit of one goal—anotHf only management valued
four. The Nets in five. Theoffered me next to nothing.
lenge would come next: a lowed interest, as did Mil-
time, however, they wouldoffer a contract above the

Not for long.   on Rockets. No thanks. The

After losing the opener l win a championship, but I
victory in Game 2 to take e.
Now if we could just win tls started in early October,

I stayed in Miami with Shannon and the kids. I was still open to the possibility of joining a team later in the season, maybe around the All-Star break, but no situation was right, and before long the Cavaliers were playing the Warriors in the 2015 Finals. That was the first time I wished I was still out there.

I didn't miss the practices, the shootarounds, the long plane rides, or the pain in my ankles every morning when I got up.

I did miss giving everything I had for something larger than myself. I will always miss that.

Soon, another season was under way, and I couldn't let go just yet. I waited to see if the right situation might pop up this time, but it didn't. In the fall of 2016, I announced my retirement.

It hit me harder than I thought it would, especially since I had not played a game in more than two years. Knowing it was now official made the reality of it all sink in. Such is the price for investing so much, for so long.

I'll always remember the day I realized, for probably the first time, that I could make it in the NBA. I was a freshman at UConn and we were at practice when Tate George, who made the heroic shot in the NCAA Tournament against Clemson in 1990, addressed the team. By this point, Tate, who came to the gym to get some work in, had played for three years in the league, with the New Jersey Nets. He had our attention.

"I'm not the most innately talented guy," he told us, "but I have been part of winning teams, and if you win, you will have a chance."

I watched him closely that afternoon. He was right. He

is also why I didn't sit home and watch the highlights on *SportsCenter,* as members of my family did. Rest on your laurels and you'll never go any further. Yesterday is over. When I wake up each morning, I ask myself: How can I win *this* day?

And in those weeks after we won the championship, I had something else to think about: *Is it time to retire?*

It wasn't the first time the idea occurred to me. During my last season with the Celtics, I bumped into Steve Kerr, the former Bulls guard and current Golden State coach, in the gym in Miami. Steve was in town to do the commentary for TNT.

"What was your process like?" I asked him. "When did you know you needed to retire?"

"I knew when I couldn't play without taking anti-inflammatories to allow my body to do it," he said.

What Steve told me really hit home. I was taking a lot of medication back then, with no sense of the long-term damage the pills might be doing to my body. The ice baths and stretching were no longer as effective, and the pounding my joints took during games and practices was almost unbearable.

Yet I didn't quit. In the end, I thought: *How can I leave these guys?* I'd been in a lot of locker rooms—some, as you know, where things got quite nasty. This was by far the best one.

The last team to win three straight championships was the Lakers in 2002. There was no reason we couldn't do the same.

LeBron was still at the top of his game, as were CB and D-Wade. Plus, the bench was as solid as ever.

In early March, we beat the Bobcats to raise our record to 43-14, although Spoelstra was driving us as hard as ever, and we always knew the team's president, Pat Riley, was a slump away from getting more involved.

The slump came all right: a loss in Houston was followed by four losses in the next five games. Riley came to practice to address the team. We sat against the wall, like in some junior high phys ed class. I don't remember what he said. Whatever it was, I'm sure he meant well, although we never got back to the level we were at prior to the slump, ending the season 54-28.

No matter. Knowing that we would make the playoffs, there was little to play for. Besides, the guys were exhausted. People always used to tell me: "You are so lucky to be in the NBA."

I would never disagree with that, but for us, this was also a job, and every job gets monotonous.

In any case, once the playoffs started, we were a different team. No longer were we flying from one city to the next and staying up all hours of the night. We stayed in one place, in pursuit of one goal—another title. First, the Bobcats fell in four. The Nets in five. The Pacers in six. The biggest challenge would come next: a rematch against the Spurs. This time, however, they would have the home court.

Not for long.

After losing the opener by 15 we fought back with a 98–96 victory in Game 2 to take the home court away from them. Now if we could just win the next two in our building, we . . .

Forget it. The next two were as ugly as the scores indicated: 111–92 in Game 3 and 107–86 in Game 4.

The Spurs were especially efficient coming out of a timeout. Popovich would get them a high-percentage shot every time, and it was not just their stars who beat us; they got major contributions from guards Danny Green and Patty Mills. The series came to a merciful end in Game 5, 104–87, Leonard with 22 points and 10 boards.

I started that game, by the way. I was one for eight, the basket coming with five minutes to go in the first quarter. A three.

The guys were pretty down afterward. We didn't expect to lose, and definitely not in five games. I sat in the locker room next to LeBron, who kept shaking his head.

In a few weeks, he'd have a decision to make—whether or not to stay in Miami—and the whole sporting world would be watching, as it had in 2010.

The whole sporting world, I don't have to tell you, would not be watching to see what I'd decide.

Once LeBron chose the Cavs, I knew I would not be returning to Miami. The question was: Would I follow him to Cleveland? He did his best to convince me, and I think he probably got tired of trying. If only management valued me as much as he did; the Cavs offered me next to nothing.

Minnesota and Memphis showed interest, as did Milwaukee, but the only team to offer a contract above the league minimum was the Houston Rockets. No thanks. The Rockets claimed they wanted to win a championship, but I knew they did not have a chance.

So, when the training camps started in early October,

I stayed in Miami with Shannon and the kids. I was still open to the possibility of joining a team later in the season, maybe around the All-Star break, but no situation was right, and before long the Cavaliers were playing the Warriors in the 2015 Finals. That was the first time I wished I was still out there.

I didn't miss the practices, the shootarounds, the long plane rides, or the pain in my ankles every morning when I got up.

I did miss giving everything I had for something larger than myself. I will always miss that.

Soon, another season was under way, and I couldn't let go just yet. I waited to see if the right situation might pop up this time, but it didn't. In the fall of 2016, I announced my retirement.

It hit me harder than I thought it would, especially since I had not played a game in more than two years. Knowing it was now official made the reality of it all sink in. Such is the price for investing so much, for so long.

I'll always remember the day I realized, for probably the first time, that I could make it in the NBA. I was a freshman at UConn and we were at practice when Tate George, who made the heroic shot in the NCAA Tournament against Clemson in 1990, addressed the team. By this point, Tate, who came to the gym to get some work in, had played for three years in the league, with the New Jersey Nets. He had our attention.

"I'm not the most innately talented guy," he told us, "but I have been part of winning teams, and if you win, you will have a chance."

I watched him closely that afternoon. He was right. He

wasn't the greatest athlete or the greatest shooter. Yet, there he was, exactly where I wanted to be.

He watched me as well.

"The freshman is better than I was," Tate said to a few others.

If he really feels that way, I thought, *I better work as hard as I can to make the most of my opportunity.*

I believe I did.

EPILOGUE

PASSING THE BATON

One afternoon when I arrived in the lot at KeyArena, I was surprised to see a car in the spot I had parked in every game day since joining the Sonics in 2003. Fine, it wasn't, officially, *my* spot; my name wasn't on the pavement. Still, I was always the first player to show up, often before our trainer, and that was the spot I picked, closest to the entrance. It was mine, and everyone knew it.

Recognizing the car, I went straight to the locker room to find my teammate Antonio Daniels.

"Dude, why did you park in my spot?" I asked him.

Antonio pleaded ignorance.

It was time for my workout. The two of us would have to talk about this later.

That night—I believe we were playing the Knicks—I scored about 40 points. I couldn't miss. In the locker room afterward, Antonio couldn't resist. "And I parked in your spot," he said, laughing. "Maybe I should park in your spot more often."

"Shut up," I said jokingly, "and never park in my spot again."

He didn't, and neither did anyone else.

I know what you are thinking: Why would I care so much about a silly parking spot?

Because one day it's a parking spot, and the next, Antonio is taking shots with me in the gym, affecting how I go through my normal workout. Before you know it, my entire routine is off, and my routine, remember, is what helped me build my confidence during my 18 years in the league, one step at a time. Show me the person who sticks to his routine, day after day, and I know he's the one you can depend on.

On a basketball team. In a law firm. In any group of people in pursuit of a common goal.

And in those 18 years, I felt a huge sense of responsibility every time I stepped on the floor.

Not just to the franchise I played for, or my teammates, my coach, or the fans. I felt a responsibility to the game, to those who came before me and to those who would come after.

I felt it my rookie year, when I was so warmly welcomed by Michael Jordan and Mitch Richmond and others who had been around for a while.

Take care of this, they seemed to be telling me, without saying those exact words. *When it's time for us to go, we will pass the baton to you. Make sure to leave the game in better shape than when you got here, and make sure you give the same speech to the next generation of players.*

No one, after all, is bigger than the game. Not Wilt, Dr. J, Michael, Larry, Magic, LeBron . . . no one. Each of us had to overcome something to get as far as we did: our background, our limitations, our doubts. Something that stopped many others and probably should have stopped us, but didn't.

A lot of times, when I was ready to give up for the day, I thought of Michael and Reggie or anyone else I measured myself against: *They're not giving up. They're still taking shots. They're still on the treadmill. I'm not giving up either.*

You don't become a champion the day you beat the other team. You become a champion the day you commit to giving your best no matter what the obstacles may be. Will you be judged? You better believe it, and the judgment might be harsher than you deserve. But that's no excuse to give anything less.

You see, I could have been like some of those kids I grew up with in South Carolina, who never thought they could make it as a professional athlete; there were, after all, no examples around town to show them the way. Instead, I realized early on that while life isn't always fair, you can't allow yourself to think that you're a victim. Or that is precisely what you will be.

Which is why today, in my early forties, I could not be more at peace. I am both a coach and an owner—a coach to my five kids, who depend on my leadership every day, and an owner to the employees who work for Grown, the organic fast-food restaurants Shannon and I opened a couple of years ago in Florida and Connecticut. In each role, I often reflect back on those people who encouraged me, in and out of basketball, and on those who tried to hold me back; the lessons from both are endless, and timeless.

As a father, I hope to prevent my four boys—Rayray, 13; Walker, 11; Wynn, 8; and Wystan, 6—and my daughter, Tierra, 25, from making poor decisions, but always keeping in mind that I can't make decisions for them, as my parents couldn't for me. And as an owner, I hope my workers know how much I care about them but also that I will hold them accountable, like those who kept me in line.

Tierra was born at a time filled with plenty of uncertainty in my life. I can still see her now, sitting in the stands at a UConn game in her Husky jacket and braids, and hear her sweet voice, "Hi, Daddy," while she waited patiently for the autograph seekers to clear out. She is strong, brilliant, and beautiful, and has always been my protector. I honor the determined child she was, and the young woman she has become.

She played Division 1 volleyball for four years and graduated from Quinnipiac University with a major in communications and a minor in management. Although she underwent two major heart surgeries for a condition that went undetected until her sophomore year, she never missed a class, or season. I'm so proud to be her dad.

The same goes for my four boys. Our oldest, Rayray, is an intense child, whether competing in track, basketball, or soccer, painting, drawing, writing a song, or building a replica of the Taj Mahal with Legos. He's incredibly competitive. He hates to lose, or maybe he just loves to win; we haven't quite figured that out yet. At the same time, he looks to help and encourage everyone around him—in the classroom or on the court. Rayray possesses a kind, loving soul, always sticking up for the underdog.

Then there's Walker, the showman, and you already know how tough he is. We like to say everything comes easily to Walker, that he excels at anything he tries. But the truth is, he's worked harder than everyone else simply to survive. He's our superhero—singer, actor, student, athlete, and a fantastic big brother—who has as much genuine enthusiasm for his siblings' achievements as his own. Walker has a heart of gold.

Our "unofficial middle child" is Wynn, who looks exactly like me. Shannon calls him "my twynn." He is smart, funny, shy, cautious, and a rules-follower. Wynn is a natural leader, setting the tone for conversations at the dinner table and in school, where he relishes every opportunity to present to the class. He, too, is quite the competitor. He loves all sports, but will say without hesitation: "Tennis is my life." Watch out, Federer, our Wynn is coming for that #1 spot!

Last, but certainly not least, is Wystan, the baby of the family, #5. He is joy personified. Wystan embodies a special spirit of wonder, possibility, and an amazing mane of hair! His name means "battlestone" in Welsh and he definitely lives up to it, with no inhibitions. I guess that's what you get when you are adored as much as he is. He goes out of his way to be a good friend to everyone in his class. We joke that he is the mayor of the boys' school because it seemed more teachers knew him as a two-year-old visitor than they knew the actual students. We are so proud and excited to see our children's bright futures unfold and which stars they

harness themselves to; for Wystan, we are convinced it will
be a supernova.

Shannon and I were going for a drive one day in Connecticut when
we passed by a playground. Three kids, about high school
age, were playing basketball. I stopped the car:

"You have room for one more?"

They sure did.

I took some shots to warm up, and it wasn't long before
they recognized me—from my days at UConn, no doubt;
this was the summer after my rookie season in Milwaukee.

Anyway, we played a game of 21, until I had to go. But
before I did, I went to the car and handed each of them a
pair of sneakers I had in the trunk. Man, I wish you could've
seen the looks on their faces.

For the longest time, I thought I had stopped for them, to
inspire these kids to keep dreaming and to believe in themselves. Truth is, I stopped for myself. For that kid on the
playground in Dalzell, who dreamed the same dream these
boys did. Who didn't have an NBA player show up one day.
Who kept dreaming nonetheless.

That kid is never far away. More than the thousands of
shots I hit in college and the pros, the shots I made in the
playgrounds remain the ones that mean the most.

There were no fans or cheerleaders. Just a group of us
playing for the pure love of the game. You win, you give
everyone high fives and take on the next team. You lose, you
sit down. And, believe me, no one ever wanted to sit down.

The best part was that what we did on those playgrounds—
and in high school, too—was not captured on video. No,

those games instead occupy a much more special place: your imagination. Whenever you did something spectacular, it spread through word of mouth, and before long, it became urban legend.

Several years ago, a stranger reminded me of a play I made in a game against West Florence during my senior year at Hillcrest. I remember it well.

My teammate, who was out of bounds, lobbed the ball to me near the rim, where I was to catch it and slam it home. We ran this play all the time. Only this time, the pass was too high and was certain to bounce off the glass.

Yet, as I jumped, it felt as normal as it could be, as if I had jumped this high my entire life. I caught the ball and threw it down. It was one of the best dunks I ever had.

"You were as high as the backboard," the guy said. "I never saw anything like it."

One day, I'm sure, I'll drive by another group of kids playing hoop in some playground, and I'll stop the car again.

I might be an old man by then, and they won't have the slightest idea who I am, but the kid inside me will still be there.

Remembering when I was like them—just me, my dreams, and the game I loved.

"You have room for one more?"

ACKNOWLEDGMENTS

So many people are responsible for the inspiration behind the writing of this book! First and foremost, I owe everything I am to my mom and dad. Through our travels as a military family, I saw the world and gained a unique perspective on people, and how to think beyond myself. Thank you, Mom and Dad!

To my siblings, John, Kim, Talisha, and Kristie; I always carry you guys with me everywhere I go. Each one of you has shaped me and helped be the man I am. I'm forever grateful for the sacrifices you have made to support my dreams. I love you.

To the teachers who have influenced my thoughts and challenged me in the classroom: Mr. Barrett, Mr. Huggins, Ms. Kypriotis, Mr. Hathaway, Mr. Brown, Mr. Barth, thank you all.

Thank you to the coaches who have taught me the skills to compete not only in sports, but in life: Jeff Lensch, Phil Pleasant, Mark Wade, Dwayne Edwards, Dale Wilson, James Smith, Karl Hobbs, Tom Moore, Dave Leitao, Howie Dickenman, Jim Calhoun, Chris Ford, George Karl, Nate McMillan, Bob Weiss, Bob Hill, Doc Rivers, Erik Spoelstra., Gerald Oliver, Armond Hill, Mike Longobardi, Tom Thibodeau, David Fizdale, Dan Craig, Octavio De La Grana, Dwayne Casey, Dean (Bustercrab) Demopoulos, Lawrence Frank, Kevin Eastman, Tyronn Lue, Sam Mitchell, and Terry Stotts. And thank you to my GMs: Mike Dunleavy, Bob Weinhauer, Rick Sund, Danny Ainge, Pat Riley.

I want to thank the strength coaches who pushed me to be stronger and healthier. Coach Martin (RIP) Tim Wilson, Dwight Daub, Bryan Doo, Bill and Eric Foran. And to the trainers: Mark Pfeil, Troy Wenzel, Ed Lacerte, Rey Jaffet, Mike Shimensky, and Jay Sabol.

I'm also grateful to the doctors: Dr. Andersen (RIP), Dr. Brian Mckeon, Dr. Harlan Selesnick, and Dr. Richard Ferkel. And to the public relations professionals: Cheri Hanson, Marc Moquin, Robyn Jamilosa, Jeff Twiss, Heather Walker, Tim Donovan, Rob Wilson, Mike Lissack. And to the equipment managers: Harold Lewis, Marc St. Ives, John (JJ) Connor, Rob Pimental.

Thank you to the military personnel at Castle AFB in California, Ramstein AB in Germany, Altus AFB in Oklahoma, RAF Bentwaters in England, Edwards AFB in California, and Shaw AFB in South Carolina—you all had so much to do with my upbringing. Thank you for showing a little kid what it means to be disciplined, respectable, and on time. Thank you to my friend Dorel Simmons. The muffler of his car was my wake-up call every morning as he was coming into my neighborhood to pick me up for school.

I especially want to thank the men I grew up playing ball against at the Shaw AFB gym with my dad and brother John. You were my biggest inspirations as a young man trying to figure out who I wanted to be.

I had so many great teammates throughout my career who have shaped how I think, and how I play basketball.

To my middle school and high school teammates: Raymond Wiltshire, Shawn Harbert, Shawn and Shannon Looney, Marc White, Deandre James, Kelvin Keith, Derrick Wright, Tee Morant, Phillip Morant, Corbin Deas, Richard Cooley, Dennis Nickens, Tony Yates, Brian Keith, Julius Gallishaw, Orvin Holliday, Berry Winn, Jamie Winn, Tyrone Dawson, Antoine Grant, Gerard and Anthony Keith.

To my brothers at UConn: Rudy Johnson, Scott Burrell, Kevin Ollie, Donny Marshall, Nantambu Willingham, Donyell Marshall, Kirk King, Travis Knight, Doron Sheffer, Eric Hayward, Jeff Calhoun, Marcus Thomas, Steve Emt, Rashamel Jones, Antric Klaiber, Dion Carson, Brian Fair, Greg Yeomans, Justin Srb, Ricky Moore, Kyle Chapman, and Ruslan Inyatkin. Thank you for challenging me and propelling me to the next level. I want to thank Tim Tolokan for all of his work as the Sports information director at UConn and Phil Chardis for taking over that role and providing me with everything I needed from my days at UConn.

I played with some incredible teammates in the NBA!

Thank you Elliot Perry, Michael Curry, Joe Wolf, Armen Gilliam (RIP), Johnny Newman, Sherman Douglas, Robert Traylor (RIP), Vin Baker, Glenn Robinson, Sam Cassell, Michael Redd, Toni Kukoc, Ervin Johnson, Jason Caffey, Jeff Nordgaard, Mark Pope, Jason Hart, Darvin Ham, Tyrone Hill, Terrell Brandon, Rashard Lewis, Antonio Daniels, Brent Barry, Nick Collison, Johan Petro, Mickaël Gelabale, Vladimir Radmanović, Ansu Sesay, Vitaly Potapenko, Reggie Evans, Jerome James, Mateen Cleaves, Damien Wilkins, Luke Ridnour, Flip Murray, Earl Watson, Kevin Garnett, Paul Pierce, Rajon Rondo, Glen Davis, James Posey, Tony Allen, Eddie House, Avery Bradley, P. J. Brown, Leon Powe, Nate Robinson, Brandon Bass, Marquis Daniels, Rasheed Wallace, Kendrick Perkins, LeBron James, Dwyane Wade, Shane Battier, Chris Bosh, Udonis Haslem, Mike Miller, Chris Andersen, Dexter Pittman, James Jones, Mario Chalmers, Norris Cole, Juwan Howard, Roger Mason—just to name a few.

Thank you to John, Jackie, Sara, Jamie, Brandyn, and Charlie Girl, for allowing me to be part of your family, and for allowing me to steal a part of you all and make her the center of my universe.

Thank you Rosalind Ramsey for teaching me how to grow up and be a man when I was just finding my way and thank you for giving me my beautiful first child, Tierra!

I want to thank every person who has rooted against me, or wished that I failed. Whoever you are, wherever you are, you kept me sharp and on my toes.

Thank you Spike Lee for believing in me enough to cast me in the movie role of a lifetime.

To my right-hand man, Orin Mayers, thank you for keeping the Allen household on point and for your continued commitment to our off-the-court success. Thank you Bianca Ramirez. Your friendship and love for the family has meant the world to us all.

Special thanks to the amazing team of professionals who cross the *t*'s, dot the *i*'s, and spend countless hours protecting my brand and creating opportunities for my future: Jim Tanner, Helen Dooley, Meredith Geisler, Lon Babby, Mike Horsey, Jon Hayes, Yolanda McBride, Rob Morris, Will Rose, and Glen "G-wiz" Parrish.

Thank you to Michael Jordan, for the inspiration that he has provided. He gave me something to strive for, someone to aspire to be like. Someone to model my life after. And thank you for picking me a long time ago to wear your shoe as one of the original members of the Brand Jordan shoe.

Thank you to everyone at Brand Jordan for keeping me in the freshest shoes anyone has ever seen. Thank you Howard White, Steve Riggins, Ric Wilson, Mark Raveling, Dale Allen, Samir Hernandez, Larry Miller, Kimo Farm, Gemo Wong, Josiah Lake, Jamal Lucas, Phil Simmons, and Tinker Hatfield.

And thanks to my community relations people: Tony Shields, Skip Robinson, Matt Wade, Matt Meyersohn, Steve Stowe. Without you guys I would've never been able to be so connected to the people in each city where I played.

I owe so much to Al, Darryl, Tamir, and Doctor D, and all my nieces and nephews, Little Tamir, Christopher, Courtney, Jamil, Little Darryl, Jade, Kayla, Kaden, and Kaleb, for spending the better part of your lives cheering me on in NBA arenas around the country—so many hours spent standing around waiting for Uncle Ray to come out of the locker room. Up way past your bedtime, no doubt.

A special thank you to my friends around the country

for supporting me, championing my career from city to city, through all the ups and downs. Thank you to: Brian Janush, Naomi Stone, Mike Rose, Ralph Giansanti, Fred Martins, Ben Zieky, Al Foreman, Gentry Humphrey, Mike Nau, Anthony Ng, Tyrone Fleming, Will Rubinow, Bobby Rosetti, Cyrus Walker, Danya Abrams, Alex Wertheim.

Of course, this book would not have been possible without the remarkable team at Dey Street Books: Lynn Grady, Benjamin Steinberg, Serena Wang, Maria Silva, and Ploy Siripant. The team was anchored by editor, Matthew Daddona, whose passion and commitment were evident from day one, and never wavered. The same goes for my agents at William Morris Endeavor, Jay Mandel, Margaret Riley King, and Carlos Fleming, who believed in the project before I had any idea of what it would entail. I also want to thank WME's Lauren Shonkoff.

As for my co-writer, Michael Arkush, it will be odd not to receive almost a daily e-mail or phone call from him. Mike brought the same work ethic to this book that I brought to the court, and I'm very grateful. I know he couldn't have made this effort without the support of his wife, Pauletta Walsh.

Last, I want to thank my beautiful wife, Shannon, for constantly keeping me focused and motivated and for providing the best, most loving environment that a man can possibly ask for, and for our awesome children. Thank you guys for being incredible and amazing in your own right!

Tierra, Rayray, Walker, Wynnie, and Wystie, let this book always remind you that life has its twists, turns, and good and bad people, but if you always believe in yourself and the direction you're headed in, you will create a life that will change the world. Your love is the thing that sustains me through life and fills me up on the inside. I love you.

ABOUT THE AUTHORS

Ray Allen, the most prolific three-point shooter of all time, played in the NBA for eighteen years, winning two championships (2008 Boston Celtics, 2013 Miami Heat). Allen, who went to the University of Connecticut, was the 1996 Big East Player of the Year. He lives in Florida with his wife and children.

Michael Arkush has written or co-written fourteen books, including *The Last Season* with Phil Jackson, *The Big Fight* with Sugar Ray Leonard, and *The Fight of the Century* about the first duel in 1971 between Muhammad Ali and Joe Frazier. Arkush was a staff writer for the *Los Angeles Times*, and has also contributed to the *New York Times* and *Washington Post*. He lives in Oak View, California, with his wife, Pauletta Walsh.